JOHN LONG
My Story

JOHN LONG

MY STORY

Published by John Long in association with Llanrhidian History Group.

First Impression – 2008

ISBN 978-0-95474-506-6

© John Long

John Long has asserted his right under the
Copyright, Designs and Patents Act, 1988,
to be identified as Author of this Work.

*Printed in Wales at
Gomer Press, Llandysul, Ceredigion SA44 4JL*

First of all, business has to be profitable
but also it has to be fun.
If you hate doing it
then don't bother to do it!.

Acknowledgements

I must thank:-

Mum for the great start she gave me in life,

Cheryl for putting up with all my varied projects over the years and Brian for his loyalty,

Pat and Martin who when asked if there was any substance in my story, gave me the encouragement and enthusiasm to finish what had started out as a ten page version of my life for my grandchildren to read after my days,

Viv, Maureen and Kenny for keeping the Contract Division ahead of our competitors,

Patrick, Jeanette and staff for the huge effort in running Homestore, and making it into the best furniture and carpet retailer in the area,

Special thanks to Colin, Sue, Bob, Jen and all at the Ashburnham Hotel, Pembrey.

And all my friends in Llanelli, Gorseinon, and Swansea – and of course, the Gower people who have meant so much to me over the last 70 years.

Contents

Chapter 1

MY EARLY YEARS

Dad died in September 1945 when I was eight years and 1 month old. It didn't seem such a big deal at the time because, after all, he was quite old in my young eyes and he always seemed to be ill in bed with a lot of bloodstained towels lying around the bedroom floor. In reality, Dad was only 38 years of age, an extremely good Golf Professional who happened to have tubercular meningitis which was incurable in those days.

After Dad died, I remember my Uncle Albie (my favourite uncle because he used to take me for rides in his lorry and make a fuss of me), taking me to one side and telling me that now my father was gone it was up to me to look after my mother and sister (he probably said the same thing to my brother Brian) and to stay close as a family. This we have done over the years and we are still close to one another sixty years on.

Mum and Dad's engagement photograph.

It is hard to remember precisely the early years but with the help of my brother Brian, we'll try to put together an accurate account of my life over the last six decades, that took me from extremely humble beginnings to where I am today – still humble but servicing an extremely large bank overdraft.

In the early 1930s my parents with my brother Brian and sister Pat lived in Clyne Valley Cottages in Killay, relatively close to Dad's work. He was an assistant Golf Professional at Clyne Golf Club.

Dad was offered the Golf Pro's job at Manselton Golf Club and the family moved to Armine Road, Fforestfach, where I was born on the 18th August 1937. I was the third child of my father Thomas Griffith and mother Lily May Long. My sister Pat was six years older than me and my brother Brian five years older. Brian recalls that Auntie Beat, (Mum's sister) announced from the bottom of the stairs, "Well, here is your new brother and he's called John." Which was

Dad at Clyne Golf Course.

a surprise to Brian and Pat, who knew nothing about pregnancies, and they assumed that Auntie Beat had found me upstairs under the bed.

Dad was also a club maker and I remember that he made me a set of clubs when I was about 5 years of age. Often when he would be giving lessons, I would trundle behind them from green to green, hitting my ball after them. If Dad had lived, then I am pretty sure that I may have ended up as a Golf Pro. I have never played a game of golf since those days but I have on a few occasions gone to a driving range and hit a few balls around, and seemingly I still have the swing.

My recollections start during the wartime, when the Germans started to bomb Swansea Docks. Dad was exempted from war service because of his past history of T.B., and continued to work in the Golf Club until it was selected as the site for an American Army camp. He then became a policeman – Police War Reservist No. 98. With the strong possibility that Swansea would be bombed, every house had been issued with an Anderson Air Raid Shelter complete with bunk beds, where, on hearing the Air Raid Warning Siren we would make our way at speed, with a torch, some food, and a chamber pot. When the 'Blitz' really started, it was a frightening three nights. Because of hasty installation the shelter had partly filled with water, so we bedded down beneath the stone slab in the pantry under the stairs. Dad was out on duty so there was just Mum, Gran and we three children. Whilst the bombers flew overhead, we could hear the bombs whistling down, and Gran would mutter "This one is for us, Lil!" Mum would tell her off for frightening us, but to us it was all a great adventure just like those of Dick Barton, Special Agent that we heard on the radio. When the 'All Clear' sounded, we went outside and looked towards Townhill which would be lit up by the fires of Swansea beyond.

Dad in his 'plus fours'.

I attended school opposite our house on Armine Road, until I was seven and then was quite shocked to find that Mum and Dad

Brian, Pat and me in Armine Road, 1941.

had decided to leave the area and we moved in the March of 1945 to the village of Llanrhidian in North Gower to take over the old pub called the Dolphin Inn. The reason behind it became apparent later on. Dad had had experience in bar management at the Golf Club and because he knew that he was very ill, he thought that they could run the pub between them and hopefully if something ever happened to Dad then at least Mum and us kids would have a roof over our heads.

During our childhood we were very close to our cousins. June Howells was the daughter of my uncle Bert and Auntie Doris. Pauline, Jean and Glynis were the daughters of Uncle Neville and Auntie Josephine. They often came to visit us when we moved to Llanrhidian.

Llanrhidian is a small village in North Gower on the edge of the salt marshes of the Burry Estuary. A steep hill leads down to the Dolphin Inn and the mill and mill pond beyond. On the village green is the Whipping Stone which is reputed to have been a pillory in former days.

Me in Llanrhidian School.

As soon as we arrived in the village I was sent to Llanrhidian Primary School and attended there until I tried and passed my 11+ exams.

It was heaven being a young boy down there in the country and I loved every minute of it. After being there for a few months, Dad's condition worsened and Mum had to run the pub on her own, doing all the cleaning during the day and in the bar every night until Stop Tap! At the same time she was taking care of Dad who was upstairs in bed which necessitated her running up and down stairs all day and night – and she never once complained.

Dad died in September 1945 and was buried in the cemetery of his choice in Oystermouth, Mumbles, Swansea overlooking the sea and the Langland Bay Golf Course.

After Dad's death, Mum wanted a photo of our remaining family. I was eight years of age, Brian thirteen and Pat fourteen. We had the photograph taken by a well known photographer – Jack Thomas in St. Helen's Road, Swansea.

From that time on we all had our jobs to do in the house. Mum was always the boss and it was up to the three of us to help her in any way possible. Pat always helped with the cleaning, and Brian and I helped with re- stocking the bar and cellar, and we washed the back and paths down with rain water that had been collected in a large water tank. Each morning we would fill a

Our family. From left: John, Pat, Mum and Brian.

large milk churn with fresh water from a tap at the side of the river and take it to back to Mum so that she would have a supply for the needs of the pub and the kitchen for the day. This would be repeated, if necessary, when we returned from school. The only toilet that we had for the pub and ourselves was at the top of the garden, and in the dark it was very difficult to climb the steps without a torch.

Each evening, we three kids used to sit in the parlour doing our homework, reading or listening to the radio. The light switches for the pub were all in the parlour and we had a system whereby at mum's request someone in the bar would knock on the connecting door. One knock meant put the bar light on, two knocks and we put the dartboard light on, and the dreaded three knocks meant that that toilet bucket needed emptying!

Brian and I took it in turns to empty the toilet buckets into deep holes dug in the garden. I did my best to get out of that job as much as possible because the sight and smell always turned my stomach. A few years later Brian signed up for the RAF and all the household jobs came on me – full time!

16

After Dad died we had a letter from the owners of the pub – Hancock's Breweries in Swansea – informing us that because Dad was the licensee of the Dolphin we would have to move out of the pub because, in their estimation there was no way that Mum could handle the pub on her own. This caused us a tremendous problem and we tried to reason with the Brewery but to no avail. They wanted us out! As luck would have it, the villagers got to know of our predicament and informed the Brewery that if they evicted Mrs. Long and her children from the pub then all the villagers would boycott the pub for evermore. The Brewery relented and gave my mother a six month trial and that trial lasted over 21 years. I will always be grateful to the villagers for this act of kindness.

When I was seven years old, my cousin Cliff Curvis, an exceptional boxer, turned professional at the age of seventeen. In his first professional fight he fought an experienced opponent named Brian Cullins and knocked him out in the second round. At the age of 19 he earned a mammoth £1,000 for a fight. That was a big milestone because you could buy three terraced houses for the same amount at that time.

To help his training and to strengthen his arms, his first job was rather unusual – rowing a large boat for men who were measuring the depth of the entrance channels all around the South and West Wales coast. He rowed all the port entrances from Port Talbot down to Fishguard and Pembroke Dock. He did his road work every morning, rowed all day then trained in the evening.

On 2nd June 1947 he fought Ronnie James at the Vetch Field, Swansea in front of a capacity crowd. He won the fight, Brian had ringside seats with my Uncle Albie but I was too young to go.

In August 1952 he fought Danny 'Bang Bang' Womba in Porthcawl and won.

Cliff beat champion Wally Thomas after knocking him out with a beautiful left hook to become Welterweight Champion of Great Britain and the British Empire.

Ronnie James on the canvas 1947.

Cliff Curvis v 'Bang Bang' Womba.

From left –Brian, Dai, Cliff, Teresa & Ken.

Today Cliff is a member of the local Commonwealth Games committee and is President of the Swansea – South West Wales Old Time Boxers Association.

Cliff never forgot his family and took great pleasure in buying a house for his Mum and Dad (Teresa and Dai.)

Even though Cliff's brother Ken was a fitness instructor and keen on boxing, it was his youngest brother Brian who was the next British and Commonwealth Welterweight Champion. He fought for the world title in the early sixties and lost the decision after a gruelling contest with Emile Griffith. But without his father Dai who was their trainer and manager they might not have achieved as much as they did. He was a strict taskmaster!

The Dolphin, June 1953 decorated for the Queen's Coronation.

Brian and I had heard lots of village stories about wild duck and geese on the marsh and one day we went out looking for a chance to catch one. A bit naïve I expect you would say, but we were only seven and twelve respectively and overall 'Townies'. We never did see any ducks – not on the ground anyway – but we did see some geese grazing, which didn't budge an inch when we approached. We singled one out and pounced on it with our sticks. I went home to fetch a sack and our pushbike and on my return we crammed the goose into the sack, loaded it onto the bike and took it home. To say that my mother was surprised would be an understatement – but as there was no going back we helped to pluck it and Mum cooked it with the warning to us all that as it was wild it almost certainly be very salty.

Dinner time came, what a sight and smell! In those days, a chicken was a real treat and we all tentatively picked at the goose, which – lo and behold – was not salty at all, and was soon gone, to make those years of wartime rationing seem like a distant memory. As soon as we were able to move, we dug the deepest hole we could and buried the evidence, but for weeks afterwards we were convinced that the police would come knocking because someone had seen us with a goose or even noticed how well fed we looked all of a sudden.

In the village, life revolved around getting home from school as quickly as possible, having a rushed tea and then going out to play with the village boys around my age. George and Eric Tucker were the first friends that I made when we moved to Llanrhidian. I remember walking up and down the hill by the post office like the Pied Piper banging a drum, with Lyn Davies, George Tucker and Alan Grove following behind. Glanville Willis was a bit younger than me but he was always ready to join us boys out in the woods – messing about as kids do. Dennis Davies and Lawrence Hixson were also part of the gang and every time we had a soccer match between us boys everyone wanted to be on the side of Donald Jeffreys because he was the best and strongest player of the lot. There was always the game of football or cricket to play (depending on the seasons) and often we would raid somebody's orchard and pinch as many apples as we could carry. It was common for us to eat so many apples that we would end up with Apple- itus! (Stomach sickness).

I was also very friendly with Roger Jones from the time that we arrived in Llanrhidian. I spent many days with him in Cillibion and he became part of the gang when he moved to The

Cross in Llanrhidian. We did have a fight one day when I bloodied his nose and he gave me a shiner, and pretty soon after that he went away to sea. It is good to see him again now after all this time and all the other boys of my era.

Llanrhidian millpond.

In the late 1940s, all of us boys in the village were always in scrapes and up to mischief. One of our favourite tricks was to roll a burning tyre from the quarry down the hill at night. The burning rubber would stick to the grass all the way down the hill, leaving a lighted trail and sometimes we would make a raft out of metal drums tied together and we would float them on the millpond – often resulting in a dipping!

We saw no danger in competing to see who could swim the fastest across one of the large pills (small tidal streams) on the marsh – with the tide surging in at a speed faster than a horse could travel.

Occasionally, word got around that the older boys would be drag-netting down in Oxwich or Llangennith Bay that night so we would all get a lift in one of the cars, or on the back of Brinley Hopkins's lorry and spend 2 or 3 hours netting for fish and hoping for a share of the mackerel or bass that were usually caught.

At that time, we were all into collecting birds' eggs and stamps and many nights we would go snaring rabbits and sometimes shooting them with an air rifle in the torchlight when it went dark. I could skin and gut a rabbit without any hesitation because they were eaten by all before myxomatosis came and spoiled our fun. After that no one wanted to eat rabbit meat.

Form photograph at Gowerton Grammar School. John Long 1st left, middle row.

When I was eleven I sat the entrance exam to go to Gowerton County Grammar School and much to my amazement I came 26th out of the 90 that passed in 1949. This put me in class 1A for the first year. From there I went into Form 2B in year 2, only to be held back in the 3rd year to Form RC. (My schooling was going downhill fast!). The children from Llanrhidian would travel on the school bus to Gowerton. Elizabeth Arnold was a favourite of mine, and so was Barbara Jones – but she was already 'spoken for' by my mate Brinley Hopkins.

One school year I sat next to Howard Morgan from Three Crosses and since that time, he has remained a friend, and I see

Gowerton School AAA Championship. John Long middle row, 5th from left. I competed in the javelin.

him occasionally. He is a thoroughly decent and able chap. Apart from being on every worthwhile committee going, he is head of the Justices of the Peace in Swansea, a County Councillor and a supporter of various charities. He has also served as Lord Mayor of Swansea.

If we are in company when we meet, he always relates the story that when we sat together at school he would always copy my answers. When, if the truth be known, I always copied his! He was one of the brightest boys in the class.

When I was twelve, Uncle Albie bought me two pairs of boxing gloves. With a punch ball fixed to the floor and ceiling in the Dolphin, some of the local boys would keep fit sparring together. We all wanted to be the next world champion!

Around the same time, I had a hand operated film projector that showed moving pictures on the plain wall. I charged one penny to see the same film night after night. Many times I would have just Alan Grove, Lyn Davies and George Tucker as the audience. After a few weeks, the novelty of moving pictures wore off – either the boys got bored with the same films or their money ran out!

In 1951 when I was going on 14, I saw an advert in the Evening Post asking for boy singers for a forthcoming Christmas Pantomime in the Grand Theatre in Swansea. Without telling my mother I attended the audition and four weeks later I had a letter out of the blue saying I was successful and asking if I would attend the first practice in Swansea. Mum was surprised and delighted and after about a dozen practice sessions we opened in the Pantomime 'Cinderella' at the Grand a week before Christmas.

The boy singers group was called 'The Silvertone Songsters' and there were twenty of us in all. Headlining the show was Gladys Morgan and Wyn Calvin and I must say we had a great time. I remember that my mother and Pat came to see the show (Brian was away in Germany in the Air Force at the time) and also a large number of the Dolphin locals came along for extra

CINDERELLA

Characters in order of appearance.

MORTALS

EGLANTINE Courtiers	Sylvia and Doreen Stephens
TOFFERINO	
DANDINI	Rhoda Diane
PRINCE CHARMING	Delya
BARON HARDUP	Wyn Calvin
MAUDIE The Ugly Sisters	Bert Cecil
ETHEL	Gladys Morgan
BUTTONS	Eddie Connor
CINDERELLA	Joan Laurie

Huntsmen, Courtiers, etc.

IMMORTALS

FAIRY GODMOTHER	Merville Tudor
DEMON KING	Frank Laurie

Fairies Gnomes, etc.

Specialities by Gladys Morgan, Eddie Connor, Sylvia and Doreen Stephens, Delya, The Borstal Boys, Rhoda Diane, The Swansea Babes and the Silvertone Songsters.

SYNOPSIS OF SCENES

SCENE	1	THE ROYAL WOODS
SCENE	2	OUTSIDE THE BARON'S CASTLE
SCENE	3	THE MORNING ROOM
SCENE	4	A CORRIDOR
SCENE	5	THE KITCHEN
SCENE	6	THE HOME OF THE BUTTERFLIES

Interval

SCENE	7	THE PALACE GATES
SCENE	8	THE ROYAL BALLROOM
SCENE	9	A CORRIDOR AT THE BARON'S CASTLE
SCENE	10	THE PALACE THRONE ROOM

Produced by JOHN D. ROBERTON, for
Scenery printed by George Flowers
Musical Arrangements for The Silvertone Songsters, by Ted Hillbourne
Dresses by Mary Bonser.

support. The lure of the greasepaint, backstage smells and show business applause has stayed with me all these years from that early age.

When I was fifteen I found that I needed to earn some extra money because the small amount of pocket money that I was getting wasn't going as far as I needed. There was a waste tip in Cillibion opposite Broad Pool where the council lorries dumped all their rubbish and I used to cycle up to the tip on my bike to collect empty Hancock's flagons because there was a 3d deposit on each bottle. I would fill a sack-full at a time and bring them

John, Pat & Brian.

Mum with Brian
in the Dolphin.

One of the many trips Mum organised from the Dolphin. This shows the wealth of characters that were frequenting the Dolphin in those days. Included in this trip are – Tony Nordoff, Roy Annetts, George Tucker, Laurence Hickson, Arthur Beynon, Fritz and Dulcie Oltersdorf, Trevor Hughes, Bob and Glenis Lucas, Gladys and Cyril Jeffreys, Bob Dallimore, May and Tom Pearce, Len Jones, Emrys Dunn, Gerald Sullivan, Mum, Brian and Dawn and Dick Beynon.

home on the bike and after washing them out thoroughly I would split the deposit with Mum 50/50.

From the age of 14 on, I helped to serve in the bar of the Dolphin every night.

In the summer holidays I used to go picking potatoes for Elwyn John, a farmer of Manselfold, Old Walls, Llanrhidian, and we would earn 1 shilling per hundredweight for every bag we picked. Once we got into the swing of it we could easily pick between 30 – 40 bags a day. That was big money to a 16 year old boy who had none. After four or five weeks not only was I used to earning money, but I was used to the strain on my back as it really was a strenuous job.

1953 was a good time for us boys to learn to dance. As learners we went to the Church Halls in Llanrhidian and Llanmadoc, dancing to the music of Ron Parry and his band. It was all foxtrots, quicksteps and tangos with a bit of line dancing thrown in. Being sixteen was certainly a time for kissing and innocence.

From left – Roger Jones, Dennis Davies and George Tucker.

Ron Parry and his band.

In 1954 I tried 7 subjects in my 'O' level examinations in school and I knew that I wasn't going to have any good results because even after some solid swatting, most of the subject matter went over my head. The result was that I passed in two subjects – Art and English Lit. Mum was terribly disappointed but I think she realised that I wasn't cut out to be an academic.

After my August results came out I made the decision that I was going to finish school and try to get a job. I called at my local Job Centre and –surprise, surprise! – I got the first job I that was interviewed for. I started work as a time and wages clerk for a company called 'Concrete Construction Ltd.' This company made and built pre-cast concrete houses in and around the Swansea area. Within 6 months I was in charge of a site office – (we built 200 houses in Portmead and Clase, Swansea) – and I was really enjoying the work.

I had also discovered a new hobby – Roger Jones and I had already explored some of the caves in Llanrhidian like Bat Hole cave which is near the churchyard stile, but in 1952 whilst playing football outside the Dolphin one morning, a car stopped and the driver asked me if I knew of any caves in the area.

In the car was a highly professional caver named Maurice Clague Taylor together with his elderly mother and two sisters Marjorie and Eileen. I joined them and took them to a small cave out under the woods called 'White Lady's Grave'. From that day onwards I spent every Saturday and

Wooley's Hole, Landimore. John Long with Maurice Clague Taylor and his sister Marjorie.

Sunday exploring and digging to enlarge passageways in various caves in the area with the Taylors.

When I first met the Taylor family they were living in a semi-detached house in Cockett, Swansea. I was often invited to their home for tea, and was amazed at Maurice's creative talents. He was a very good artist and had many of his large paintings and a fantastic collection of Egyptian and Indian artefacts scattered around his rooms. One large ruby-studded silver headpiece hung on the wall, and one day, when he was cleaning it he must have touched a secret lever as a portion of it opened to reveal a concealed hiding place. Inside was a cloth pouch containing a white substance that Maurice claimed was a deadly poison stored by the original owners many hundreds of years ago for use if their lives were ever in danger!

Maurice also made wonderful galleons in full sail and wrote articles for various publications – his favourite subject was obviously caving. He loved swimming and would swim and dive locally in Cockett pond (sometimes in a wet suit) – no matter what the season. At the bottom of his garden was a large glasshouse that contained a magnificent collection of cacti of all shapes and sizes and he also had a large pond containing dozens of huge carp and goldfish. He also loved to sunbathe in the nude in his back garden – much to the horror of his next door neighbour! To him this was a perfectly natural state to be in.

A year after meeting Maurice and his family, I was in Llethryd one day and could see the river going underground and re-emerging a few miles down the valley in Parkmill. Because of the minor success that was achieved in the White Lady's Grave, I decided to see how far I could follow the river underground. It was quite difficult on first entering the cave because, due to the quantity of water rushing through the small entrance and passageways, there had obviously been roof collapses, leaving it quite dangerous in certain areas. At that time I decided to wait for the warmer weather, when the movement of water would be a lot less.

On my next visit I was amazed to see that not only had the river practically dried up, but on entering the cave I found that since my last visit the water had changed course leaving quite an interesting passageway for me to explore. After about 200 yards, the way on seemed to be a bit higher than the river level and this necessitated quite a lot of climbing and scrambling along many little caverns with stalagmite and stalactite formations everywhere. My torch picked out some brilliant 'bacon-like' flows, and thousands of stalagmites and stalactites of pink and blue and yellow, in various sizes and thickness (some 100ft. long) filled my eyes. I realised I had found something special. The main cavern itself was huge. I tried to shine my torch across and upwards and I couldn't see the extent of it either way. In my estimation it could take the Guildhall in Swansea within it quite easily. It was truly magnificent and the find of a lifetime!

The following day, Maurice and his family came down to see what I had found. I have never seen anyone so excited, because he had been potholing for years, and here was a 16 year old boy giving him the moment that he had dreamt of.

The Taylor family spent a few years photographing and plotting whenever the water levels allowed entry to Llethryd Swallet, and wrote a number of articles about this special find. A few years later, I joined the RAF and shortly afterwards the cave was closed due to a serious accident to a person not used to the dangerous levels and roof falls.

Maurice later prepared two volumes of photographic records of the caves at Llethryd Swallet, which he described as the best decorated in Wales. These two books were his remarkable testimony to the wonders of the caves that we had explored and after

his days I was thrilled to find that he had bequeathed them to me. The accompanying photographs are all from his books. To the inexperienced caver however, the Grand Cavern is now lost forever.

Photographs of Llethryd Swallet.

Chapter 2

CALLED UP

I went in a boy and came out a man!

I met my first wife Ann when I was seventeen, and after a few weeks of knowing her distantly, I took her to the pictures in the Tivoli Cinema, Gowerton. This was the regular Saturday night date for months to come, and I was soon introduced to her mother and father Julie and Les. Les had his own milk round in Loughor, Swansea delivering milk from 5 a.m. until 10.30 a.m., except for a Friday when they collected the money for the week. Les and Julie rarely finished before 7 p.m. on a Friday.

After knowing Ann for about 6 months I started staying at her home on weekends and because it was a three bedroomed house, all the bedrooms were taken with Les and Julie in one room, Ann in her room and her brother Huw in his own room. I ended up sleeping on the floor downstairs in the dining room. It was rather awkward when Les started his 5 a.m. shift on the milk, so it became the norm that I got up at the same time as him on a Saturday and Sunday morning and I helped him with his deliveries. Now, with both of us running around we were finished and back home by 9.30 a.m. – ready for an early second breakfast. At that time I was known as John the Milk!

My weekends of caving were suddenly put on the back burner with the opposite sex having more of a priority, and Maurice and Co. were relegated to either a fine summer's night or the odd Sunday morning.

In August 1955 I received the dreaded letter from the government saying that I was to be called up to do my National Service. Brother Brian had already signed up for three years in the R.A.F. so I applied to go in the R.A.F. and had an I.Q. Test and somehow or other I was accepted and told to report to Cardington RAF Camp, Bedfordshire on the 18th October 1955, for 'Kitting Out'. On the same train from Swansea (High Street) Station and sitting in the same reserved carriage was another Swansea lad going to the same camp. John Murton Nethell (Chunky) was his name and we have been friends since that day.

After 7 days of collecting our kit and acclimatisation to the strict regime, we were both sent to RAF Padgate to do our 8 weeks of square bashing. Those weeks were certainly hard and regimental. We were awoken at 6.30 a.m. every morning and because it was a particularly hard November, many times our socks were frozen to the windowsills. The billet was always cold with all of us huddled around a single coal stove in the centre. When we changed to go to bed we all covered our beds with, not only our blankets but our greatcoats and uniforms to give us that extra bit of warmth.

Kit inspections happened every week and we would spend every evening bulling up our black boots and also pressing our uniforms and ironing our own shirts and underwear. If our kit wasn't up to standard or our bed blankets not folded to perfection we were given extra duties to do late into the night. I remember two of the boys in the billet answering back the Drill Instructor Corporal only to end up brushing the parade ground with their toothbrushes.

There was a lot of pressure on us to learn the drill and rifle moves quickly and many evenings we would be practising them in the billet, each one of us helping the other, making sure that we all got it right the next day. For boys, only 18 years of age, probably the first time being away from their family, under pressure and cold, it was quite an ordeal. So much so that it all got on top of one of the lads in the next billet and he ended it all by committing suicide. The corporals had kept picking on him and he was found hanging from a clothes hook in the toilet block.

Throughout our 8 weeks training we were given various tests, one of them was in the firing range. We had target practice of 200 yards from the circle and had to get four bullets within the centre circle to get what everyone wanted – the Cross Rifles Badge sewn on our uniform arm. No problem! Because I was brought up from a young boy to shoot rabbits I came top of our billet, and I was very proud to sew on and wear the arm Cross Rifle motif.

Six boys in our billet. Don Evans is to my left.

RAF Padgate was a camp just outside Warrington and after being confined to camp for the first six weeks we were let out one weekend to go to the local dance. The annoying thing was that also in the Warrington vicinity was an American Air Base and the Yanks also went to that Saturday dance and because they were a lot more smartly dressed in their gabardine uniforms than us in our drab woollen uniforms, they had all the luck with the local Lancashire lasses. They were on five times the amount of pay that we were having (twenty eight shillings less seven shillings that was automatically sent home to my mother every week) so really we were no competition to the brash American Airmen and there was no chance of walking any girls home.

During my last two weeks before our Passing Out Parade, I was told to report to the guard house at an early hour in the morning. Evidently a Flight Lieutenant Officer had died in Camp and I was going to be one of the six airmen to act as Guard of Honour. We fired blanks into the air over the graveside as a tribute when the coffin was being lowered into the ground. It was quite an honour to be selected out of thousands of Airmen that were billeted on the site and I shall always remember the experience.

Also in the last two weeks we were given more aptitude tests and we had to apply for wherever we wanted to go after finishing Square Bashing. Of course, like everyone else I applied for an overseas posting and what do you know – I got posted to R.A.F. St. Athan, only 50 miles from home. The only people who were pleased were my mother and my girlfriend because it meant that I would be home most weekends.

Home at last! Nine weeks away from home and it seemed like a year! What a lovely change to come home to a warm house and to some good home cooking again – and my mum.

Christmas went by in a flash and in the first week of January 1956 I reported to my new camp posting. Two weeks after settling in I was again transferred to the western side of the camp, (the camp was 32 square miles in size) to the 32 M.U. RAF St. Athan's. This camp was the Maintenance Unit for the U.K. RAF maintaining all service aircraft.

On my posting I was upgraded from A.C.2 Grade (Aircraftsman 2) to an A.C. 1, which gave me an extra seven shillings a week. I joined the Pay Accounts Department and it was my job to be in charge of the wages of about 200 Airmen. There were in all about 15 of us in the Accounts Dept. and over the next 21 months we all became lifelong friends. I meet and correspond with many of them today. All of them seem to have got on rather well in life so the grounding that we had in the RAF couldn't have done any of us any harm.

Of all my mates in the RAF 'Spike' Roy Jones was probably

the closest followed by Don Evans, 'Ianto' John Roberts, Geoff Ash and Ed Hawkins. These five were extremely talented boys. Spike was a qualified accountant, Don was an estate agent and valuer, Ianto was a highly talented pianist, Geoff the camp photographer and Eddie worked in advertising. All ended up after their National Service doing what they were trained to do. Spike joined a number of P.L.C.s in London as a financial accountant, ending up as Financial Director of Thorn Electrics, Australia. Don Evans took over from his uncle as head of Chris John & Co., Valuers in Cardiff. Ianto was a music master in a college in Pontypridd and Eddie was a designer near Fleet Street in London.

During our stay at St. Athan, we were all extremely fit. Every night was spent either in the gymnasium or the full size swimming pool. Spike was County Class in tennis and

Ianto at the piano, with Keith (Cam) Cameron from Gorseinon on his left.

table tennis so that meant I would take a heavy beating from him in either of those sports. I was a better runner and swimmer than he was so at the end of the night it was down to which one of us was the better boxer to decide the overall winner of the night.

Every week somebody was either leaving camp for somewhere else or coming to the end of their National Service and this was just the excuse that we all needed for a demob party. These drinking sessions were always held at the White Hart in Llantwit Major, being at that time one of the nearest pubs to the camp and also because it had a good upright piano that was in tune. We always had Ianto to play the piano and many times we would sing ourselves hoarse, making a hell of a lot of noise singing all the local hits of the time – Frankie Lane's numbers etc. and later we turned to some of Elvis's songs and skiffle (Lonnie Donegan) was also a specialty.

Don had a banger of a car, an old Austin 7 that we used to commandeer for every outing and it was not unusual to have seven or eight of us crammed into the car to go to the pub. Most nights after stop tap there were far more going back to camp than we had going to the pub.

On one occasion, we were rather high on alcohol when we left the pub at about 11 30 p.m. (We had to be in camp by 12 o'clock although many times we sneaked in over the fences if it was much later.) There were eight of us in the car all singing rather loudly, going hell for leather through the lanes from Llantwit Major to the camp, when on rounding one of the bends in the lane we hit something in the middle of the road. After stopping and reversing back to the incident area we found a pair of shoes in the middle of the road and heard a groan from the other side of the high hedge. It turned out that we had knocked another RAF Airman right over the hedge as he was walking back to camp. He was perfectly O.K. – (that's what he said!) so we ended up with 9 people having a lift to the camp. All very intoxicated Airmen!

Because we were in charge of the pays and payroll of West Camp, between us all we were into all the scams and skives going! We didn't have to do any of the weekly parades to the annoyance of all the ordinary airmen. We always had priority for meals in the cookhouse and always ended up having extras whenever we wanted them. Also we usually made a visit to the cookhouse late at night whenever we were hungry. (Many trips after a night on the beer) and were always given what we wanted because we were the boys in charge of everybody's pay.

Spike had a Velocette 2 stroke scooter and I always went with him to all the local dances in Penarth (Bingles) and Cardiff (the Victoria Ballroom) whenever we could make it (as long as it didn't clash with someone's Demob party!) On many occasions we would see the same girls going to the dances each time and it ended up with Spike meeting a girl called Dianne (Dee) from Cardiff and the result was that he married her and moved to London two weeks after me. They are still married today and live in Australia!

Four weeks before I was due to be demobbed I saw an advertisement in the Cardiff Echo newspaper showing that auditions were being held for Hughie Green's 'Opportunity Knocks' in the Park Hotel in Cardiff with the winning act to go to London to appear on the Radio Show. Ianto accompanied me and I played 'Birth of the Blues' on the harmonica. The adjudicators told me (like everyone else) that they would get in touch.

Two weeks later I was told to contact a London telephone number because I was going to be on the radio in Hughie Green's 'Opportunity Knocks' that weekend. So Ianto and I were rushed to Baker Street, London to a studio called London Studios. We had five minutes rehearsal with the band and we were then live on radio that night.

Everyone in the camp and at home was listening to the show that night. We had a lot of applause in the studio but I came second. (I had no chance of winning on that occasion. The winner was a beautiful young girl singer who definitely was a 'friend' of Hughie's and had it sewn up from the start!). Still, it was my second time before a large audience and after this show I knew that I wanted to be in Show Business.

Over the last six months in the RAF we formed a skiffle group in our billet and I played guitar and harmonica (not at the same time!)

The actual recording of me playing the harmonica on Hughie Green's 'Opportunity Knocks' broadcast October 1957.

Ianto, when he had finished in the RAF, went to teach music during the day in Pontypridd College and he played gigs in the evenings – even joined Tom Jones (before he was famous) and ended up playing on HTV and writing scores for the orchestras in college. He was and still is extremely talented but sadly, fifty years on his sight is impaired. Ianto still plays the organ in church because, as he tells me, "I have played all the hymns over the years and know them all by heart".

October 18th 1957, I was demobbed from the RAF. I told my mother that I was going straight to London to seek my fame in Show Business.

My demob party.

I organised a reunion for my RAF friends when Spike came over from Australia to visit us. From left –Spike, me and Ianto.

Chapter 3

TIN PAN ALLEY

I was recommended to go to a Mrs. James, 77 Sussex Gardens who had a large guest house to see if she would put me up 'long term'. She was a nice, elderly Welsh lady from Porthcawl and she gave me a room at the top of the house for 3 guineas a week, room only. She ran the guest house with her son and daughter-in-law and they were always very nice to me. Next door in Sussex Gardens lived the American couple Ben Lyons and Bebe Daniels – both very pleasant people. They starred with their son Richard and daughter Barbara in the radio comedy programme 'Life with the Lyons' in the 1950s.

I had a total savings of £80 and that was to last until I became famous! I had a small electric ring in my room and every night I boiled myself a tin of soup and made myself a sandwich. Sometimes on the weekend Mrs. James would invite me to have Sunday lunch with them because she could see that I was on the 'bread line'. I'd eat as much as possible because that was going to be the best and biggest meal for maybe a fortnight.

I used to rehearse the harmonica in my room every day but had to keep quiet if I stayed in at night because it annoyed the people staying there. Over the first month I went to various auditions to try to get work, and had cards printed with 'Johnny Long, harmonica player' and Mrs. James's telephone number. Pretty soon it was obvious that I was up against my harmonica idols – Max Geldrey, Tommy Reilly and Larry Adler, so if there was any work that came from the agents then they were always the first to get the job. Let's face it – nobody had heard of Johnny Long! Every day I would go to Tin Pan Alley (Denmark Street) looking for work. After three weeks I gave up the idea of majoring on the harmonica and made the decision that to get anywhere I **had** to play the guitar, so I spent all my savings on a Blonde Hofner Guitar. Now I really was on the breadline!

One of the agents in Tin Pan Alley recommended that I went to the 2 i's Coffee Bar where sooner or later he thought I would 'click'.

The 2 i's was a coffee bar on the ground floor in Denmark Street, Soho and to the right hand side was a small staircase going down to a rather dingy basement area. To the back of the basement was a small stage area that could just about accommodate four people with one mike stand. The rest of the basement area was standing room only, and when it was full (and most nights it was bursting with youngsters) it could accommodate about a hundred people. Everybody paid two shillings to get down the stairs and stand in a very smoky, claustrophobic atmosphere to watch the local band of the time and see and hear all the possible new stars that emerged from the place.

The resident band at the time was a skiffle group called 'The Vipers Skiffle Group' (formally it was Wally Whyton and the Vipers until Wally left them to make his own career in Radio and Television as a presenter.) Their bass player had a pet monkey. Many times it would sit on his shoulder during his set. By the end of 1957 the skiffle craze had passed and the group left the 2 i's as it then changed to a rock and roll venue.

I was quickly a regular at the 2 i's and most nights I played and sang with the band from 8 pm until 2 am. After finishing the night I would walk from Soho to Sussex Gardens (I couldn't afford the taxi fare) where I had my own key to get in at around 3 in the morning. Every day I would try to get a gig somewhere so that I could try to get some money together, but after about six weeks and the purchase of a second hand guitar I was completely broke.

I had to sign on the dole to get some income that I could rely on to pay for my accommodation, but that meant that I had to go for job interviews. A glut of jobs were offered me and after turning down about a dozen, I took a daytime job – 9 am to 5 pm in an Accounts office in Fleet Street with a company called Alfred Bates Advertising. Working every day 9-5 in the office and every night 8-2am at the 2 i's was very tiring but I was only twenty years old and I had the energy to do it.

During this time I started to write and sing my own songs and wrote a song called 'All over you' which was a close harmony song like the popular Everley Brothers songs of that time. I was recommended to take the song and sing it for a man called George Elrick, who was an agent and had his own hourly show on radio. After I had finished, he said that he was positively interested in handling the song for me as long as I signed an agreement that the song was written by George Elrick and Johnny Long. I was promised only 50% of the royalties that would have come from it – all the rest was to go to him! I never signed the agreement and the song was never published. In fact he made the threat that if he didn't handle the song then nobody would take it in Tin Pan Alley – and nobody did take it because it was quite a closed shop in those days and I was very young and green.

In February 1958 I noticed in the 'Wanted' portion of the Melody Maker an advert for a harmonica player. I rang the advertised number and was asked to go for an interview at an address in Denmark Street. I was auditioned by a 'Mr. Mills' and played him a number of songs and also played the record of the Radio Show with Hughie Green. The Morton Frazer Gang who were booked for a country-wide tour of all the Moss Empire halls had lost one of their lead players, and they were desperate to find a replacement. I passed the audition and was offered £10 a week with all accommodation and travelling expenses included, on the condition that I started with the group the following Monday in a Moss Empire venue in Brighton. Unfortunately I couldn't join them at such short notice because I was getting married two weeks later and had booked a honeymoon in Paris. So I had to pass up on that opportunity. About five years later I found that 'Mr. Mills' turned out to be Gordon Mills who was the manager of Tom Jones and Englebert Humperdink; he made a fortune for all three of them!

I had also met Bruce Forsyth at a music publisher's office in Tin Pan Alley, where he was promoting a record that he had just made called 'I'm in charge!' This was his catchphrase on Sunday Night at the London Palladium. He had progressed from being a concert party comedian to compering one of the biggest shows on television in the 1950s and early 1960s.

Later that month, I had a call from my agent with a booking for me on a TV pilot show called 'Saturday Hop'. The show had many stars in it – Marty Wilde, Josephine Douglas, The Kay Sisters etc. and it was recorded on a Sunday at the Café de Paris

Brian's stag night
at the Dolphin.
Brian second right.

in Regent Street but sadly it was never transmitted. In the order of play I was written into the script as Johnny Luck and for my first time in a TV recording it was very interesting to be among some of the big TV names. Alas the pilot show never took off and the positive guarantee of six shows came to nothing.

I made a brief return to Llanrhidian for Brian's marriage to Dawn in 1958. His stag night party was held in the Dolphin.

During my time at the 2 i's Coffee Bar I made friends with some guys from Grantham, Lincs. and we played together for about a month until two of the boys made the Big Time. One was called Ray Taylor who was taken up by the pop 'Svengali' Larry Parnes – he changed his name to Vince Eager and he ended up on the 'Six Five Special', 'Oh Boy!' and 'Drum Beat' TV shows. The other boy to make good from our group was called Liquorice Locking – a bass player and he found fame by being a member of Cliff Richards' Shadows and one of his first gigs was in the film 'Summer Holiday'. Since that time he has turned to religion and is now a Jehovah's Witness.

One of my London gigs.

49

It was a difficult time trying to juggle my hours between my advertising job and evening work, as well as trying to get as well known as possible –and taking every gig that I could get. One night I appeared in a club called the New Bagatelle Club in Mayfair. As soon as I went onstage I could hear voices in the darkened audience saying – "that's John Long from the Dolphin!" It turned out that there were thirty women there from the New Moon Club in Llanrhidian on a trip to London and happened to be in that club on that night. I ended my set singing 'We'll keep a welcome in the hillside' and all the Welsh audience stood up and joined in. It was a great night!

On the 'Six Five Special' I sang one of my own songs called 'All over you' but it didn't work as it was too much of a ballad, so the publishing company put forward their suggestion of Gun Law. I have since tried to obtain a copy of the show only to be told that all the early recordings were scrapped after a time, so I have nothing to show of my TV engagements. My show business memorabilia, my Blonde guitar and personal recordings were lost or seriously damaged after the breakdown of my marriage (as can be seen from the state of some of my recordings), and thrown into a shed.

Gun Law recorded in Denmark Street.

Pipe of Peace. 78 rpm. This is a demo disc of a new song given to me by a Tin Pan Alley Publishing Company.

All Over You. My first record of the Long Brothers. Recorded in Regent Sound, Denmark St. London.

If Dreams came true.
My 3rd recording at
Regent Sound.

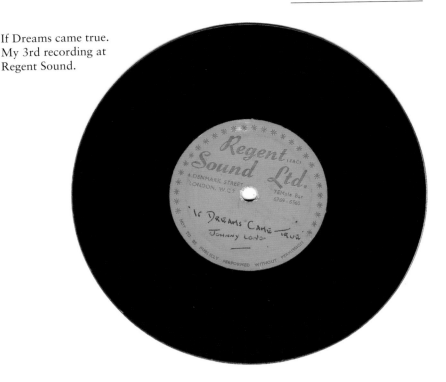

During the spring of 1958 my friend Spike from the RAF was demobbed and he also relocated to London. On many occasions he spent his nights with me at the 2 i's acting as my agent, touting for business amongst the most likely looking talent agents that used to come to the shows every night. Most nights there was a little boy who would stand in front of the stage and grab your ankle when you were singing, asking 'Can I please sing, mister?' He was an exasperating nuisance all the time! It turned out a few years later, that this kid ended up becoming the rock star Gary Glitter, only to lose face in recent years when he was convicted of being a paedophile. He was sentenced to a long time in a foreign gaol.

It was not unusual to see half a dozen stars of the day return to the 2 i's in the evening. I recall one night there was great excitement among the crowd. That night we had Wee Willie Harris, the Most Brothers, Terry Dene, Marty Wilde, Vince Eager, Joe Brown and many more who all performed a few numbers with the band. They were all part of the Package Show put together by Larry Parnes and were obviously appearing in a venue close to Soho.

My girlfriend Ann who was living in Loughor, Swansea at the time, didn't like the idea of me being in London on my own, living it up while she was at home in Wales, and she wanted to get married as soon as possible. We were married in March 1958 and she came to live with me in a flat in Sydenham Hill, S.E. London. She got a job in Fleet Street also as a secretary so at least we had another regular wage coming in.

When my RAF friend Eddie Hawkins was demobbed from the RAF he made contact with me in London and he also got a job in advertising near Fleet Street. We got together a few nights a week appearing as 'The Long Brothers' and made a recording of my song 'All over you'. In the summer of 1958, I organised a Rock

& Jazz Boat down the Thames. I advertised in the 'Melody Maker' for acts and bands to play on the boat and had quite a few replies. Of course, 'The Long Brothers' were topping the bill. It was a sell-out evening and one that I will always remember.

At that time it was unheard of to have a Rock Music Thames trip. We were ahead of our time!

Alexis Korner.

I had met Alexis Korner in late 1958 when he was appearing in a show called Saturday Club. He was originally a solo folk singer, and later formed a 'blues' group. Over the next three years I became quite friendly with him and his wife Bobby. They invited Ann and me to have dinner with them at their Queensway apartment with the main topic of conversation being 'how to get ahead in show business!'

Money was certainly getting more plentiful and what with TV shows, gigging and both of us working full time, I was able to put some of it into a small furniture manufacturing business venture in partnership with a guy that I had known about six months named George Budge. After a short period of time I realised that George was selling some of our goods on the side for cash and pocketing the proceeds, so I confronted him and under the threat of putting it into the hands of the police he gave his job up and vanished into thin air.

From that time on, we started manufacturing tubular steel kitchen sets and stools. I ran the manufacturing business from a garage in Ilford, and soon we were buying goods from the East End of London – Shoreditch and Hackney Road. To help give us a bigger range of goods, I started marketing them under our own name –'Dolphin Products'.

My Dolphin logo.

Most of our suppliers were Jewish and after trading with me for a few months I started having a good name for reliability and payment and in most cases I was given credit, which was practically unknown in those quarters at that time.

Later we moved to bigger premises in Ilford and the business began to expand. All this time I was still gigging in the evenings and saw very little of my wife during the week. She began to get homesick for Wales and always hated the life we were leading in London. I had an aunt in Bromley, Kent who ran a large guest house. At the bottom of her street there was a large house for sale for £1,100 which she said would make a lot of flatlets and she advised me to go for it. Ann was definite that she did not want it because it meant that our London episode would be a permanent stay if we had taken it. So I was talked out of it. Returning home from work one night later, we opened the door only to be met with water everywhere. There had been a leak upstairs above our accommodation and it had brought all the ceilings down. We were so upset by the mess and upheaval that a decision was made to pack up and relocate back to Wales. I sold the stock in the business – let my right-hand man have all the contacts – and within two weeks we were back where Ann always wanted to be – Loughor, Wales.

At the same time that we left London, Spike and Dee left for Australia, Eddie Hawkins left for Canada and Geoff Ash, who had done all my photo publicity and really helped me by not charging me for any work that he had done) became very big in the photographic field in London. He photographed Twiggy and rubbed shoulders with Lord Litchfield. He befriended James Hunt (Formula 1 racing driver), Peter Sellers, Lord Snowdon and many more and all this within three years of me returning to Wales. I knew I should have stayed!

It seems that the lure of show business runs in my family. My Auntie Beatrice was a show girl (dancer) touring with the Moss Empire, where she met and married my uncle Billy. He was a baritone and pianist. They had a son Des and a daughter Freda. Des was very talented and in the 1940s he appeared under the name of 'Des Williams' on the Variety Bandbox and Welsh Rarebit radio shows. He also played the saxophone and eventually had his own 20 piece orchestra – the 'Des Williams Orchestra', where he fronted the band and wrote all the scores. During the late '50s he moved to the Canary Islands, where he owned a fantastic night club that featured him and part of his band. From there he moved to South Africa where he was a big name on radio and television. He died last year at the age of 79.

His sister Freda married Reg and they adopted two children. One daughter Sue married Colin and had three children. Their son Ollie Middleton is now a drummer in a band called 'Zico Chain' who are Number One in the heavy rock charts as I write this!

Ollie with Cheryl and me.

Chapter 4

BACK HOME

What do I do now?

Back home in 1961, I didn't have a job and I didn't know what I wanted to do. We stayed with Ann's mother, father and brother until we bought our first house in Cecil Road, Gowerton. It was a nice house and had a rather large garage and cellar. Ann got a job as a medical secretary in Morriston Hospital and at the same time I got a job as assistant secretary to the Road Haulage Association in Cardiff. This meant me travelling every day to Cardiff by train to spend the day in the most boring job on earth. I stuck it out for 3 months and decided that I couldn't take it any more and I gave my notice.

Three Cliffs Bay transformed into Tangiers.

I saw an advert in the Swansea Evening post for Extras for a film that was being made at Three Cliffs Bay on the Gower Coast and my brother Brian and I turned up and we were both taken on. The film was called 'The Inspector' starring Stephen Boyd and Dolores Hart. The first week of filming we were dressed up as modern day gunrunners in a gunboat which ended up being stuck on a sandbank out in Swansea Bay.

Extras in 'the Inspector' – Brian left and me on right.

It made newspaper and TV headlines because we were all rescued by the Mumbles Lifeboat, all twenty of us dressed in our outfits. During the second week I did one scene dressed as a stand-in for Stephen Boyd, and the third week the filming sadly came to an end with us all dressed as Arabs. On the 8th October 1962, 'The Inspector' opened in the Carlton Cinema in Swansea and I think everybody from the town was there to witness all our acting debuts. It ran for six days only. Unfortunately our parts were only in the last ten minutes of the film, so if you nodded off for a few minutes during the film there was every chance that you would easily miss us and the Gower coastline!

During the early 60s, I bought a second hand Bedford van and started to bring furniture from London to wholesale to all the local furniture stores around South and West Wales. I also decided to buy an old 12 ft. caravan to hitch up to the van. I stripped the interior out of the caravan and made it into a touring showroom. There was one slight problem however. The caravan was far too heavy for the Bedford van to pull.

I made an appointment to visit a small furniture shop in Maesteg with my show van. Instead of going to Bridgend and then over to Maesteg, I made the fatal mistake of travelling to Port Talbot and up over the mountains via the Bryn. Halfway up the mountain, after struggling laboriously, the van suddenly surged forward and I realised that I had lost my caravan! Somehow it had pulled away from my hitch and the last I saw it was careering down the road and over the mountain. Everything was smashed to pieces – so I never made my appointment! I was too embarrassed to tell people how stupid I had been.

Mrs. Rees from Hillend Caravan Site, Llangennith, Gower asked if I could supply her with 200 surf boards (belly boards).

Hillend caravan site, Llangennith, overlooking Rhossilli bay.

So I had them cut to size 4ft by 1 ft. and had them steam pressed to make the front bend and then had them rounded. They were made of marine ply and painted red. From my sample I sold 200 to a gift shop in Rhossilli and 400 to Atkinson's Sports Shop in Oxford Street, Swansea. Orders came rolling in from Tenby and Caswell Bay and before you knew it I was in the summer sports item business.

My garage and cellar couldn't cope with the quantities, so I bought an RAF sectional hut 100 ft. x 20ft. from Pembrey, dismantled it and re-erected it on a small bit of land that my father-in-law owned in the Quarry, Loughor. Business expanded overnight.

I had an order from every large Co-op in South Wales for plastic pedal bins. I bought 50,000 from the manufacturers unassembled and had every household in the street assembling these and putting them in dozen bags. We paid everyone by piecework and even had Tom, the local headmaster assembling them. I am still reminded of these bins today, forty years afterwards, with great affection.

After the success with our pedal bins, I decided to go to Cologne, Germany to a trade show, because things were so much cheaper on the continent than over here. While at the show I was made sole distributor of 'Hastrup' ironing boards for the U.K. and ordered a 40ft container from Denmark right away. Also in one corner of this Great Exhibition I came across a company from Austria manufacturing wheelbarrow concrete mixers and tractor mixers. At that time there was no one making these in this country so I sewed up a distribution agreement for the whole of Great Britain. (The company was called Alois Kober KG.)

My first consignment of mixers came to us within 4 weeks and we sold out before they arrived. I ordered 100 mixers for my second load and had also pre-sold them before they left Austria. Unfortunately, they were shipped over during the Dockers' Strike in London, and were left for 12 weeks in the open in all weathers on the dockside. By the time that they were delivered to us they were all rusty and had to be repainted before we could sell them.

I now had a problem. The mixers were starting to take off in a big way, also the furniture and ironing boards were being bought like hot cakes and unfortunately I was so full of stock at home in my garage, in Loughor my father-in-law's garage and large shed were full, and also our new sectional building in the Quarry was also bursting at the seams – I needed a larger premises.

After weeks of searching I found an empty brick building to let at Spring Mills, Berllwyd, Penclawdd. It was 2,000 sq. ft. with an outside office and toilet. Now I could relocate from all my sheds and garages to one building.

Spring Mills, Penclawdd.

Within weeks the warehouse was full also, but because of the height of the building there was room to put in an extra floor. In fact, over the next six months I put in two floors, so that gave me 6,000 sq. ft. Because I had so much more room I diversified to all types of furniture and carpets and at the same time increased our staff to seven people.

I sold my rights of the concrete mixers for Great Britain to a company in Wolverhampton purely because as a company we could not mix machinery with furniture. The company that bought my idea is still in existence today, worth many millions of pounds making their own range of products, importing and exporting, and the barrow mixer is more popular than ever. You will see it in every major DIY store and Builder's Merchants in Britain.

One Friday morning, two plain clothes policemen turned up at the Spring Mills, Berthlwyd warehouse asking if they could speak to me personally. It turned out that they had been given a tip off from a local 'grass' that there was going to be a break-in at our warehouse that night. They asked us if they could put two policemen inside the building that night and said they would also keep an eye in the building on the outside, from the bank above the Berthlwyd Inn.

We left the warehouse at 5.30 pm. after locking in the police as night watchmen and evidently, about 6.30 pm. thieves broke in through the asbestos roof on the lower part of the building and were apprehended by the inside security coppers. One of the intruders did in fact escape over the marsh behind the warehouse but he was arrested after crossing ditches and pills near Loughor Bridge – very wet and caked in mud! The three men were put on trial for attempted burglary; two were fined and one was sent to prison (he had a record!).

One of my friends, Wyn Hopkins, worked for the N.C.B. in the survey department. He had inside knowledge that, because of the Abervan disaster, the coal tip at Garngoch was going to be levelled by the N.C.B. and there were going to be plots of land available for commercial development. I purchased three acres of land fronting the main road and waited for the mound of coal on my land to be levelled. As there was a deep mine shaft on my land, the N.C.B. filled it in with most of the tip. The land cost £3,000 which in those days was a great amount of money to a small business, but after speaking to Stan Burnhill, my friendly bank manager, I had his assistance to go ahead. Later on I bought a further acre of land (No Man's Land) on the top side of our back land from the estate for £50 because it was only accessible from our land so no one else wanted it.

I sat on the land for one year but because our Berllwyd unit was going so well it was important that I kept the momentum going so I applied for a building to be put on our land. This time 10,000 sq. ft. with an office and toilet block attached. I formed John Long Furnishers Ltd. and started wholesaling 'Schreiber' furniture to the whole of Wales. In fact our wholesaling was so successful that Schreiber Furniture used our system as a franchise throughout the whole of Great Britain.

John Long Furnishers.

In 1970, I decided to buy the Glen Ballroom and 'Scot Lanes Bowling Alleys' in Llanelli from a likeable character called Davey Scott. This was the largest privately owned ballroom in Wales and it had a large ballroom, nightclub, restaurant and ten lanes of bowling alleys. It also had a revolving stage in the main ballroom – one of only two in Wales at that time.

I also took on all the staff that had been with Dave over the previous ten years. I retained the manager Mike John and made him the working director and without him I would have sold it

The former Glen Ballroom.

long before I did. We were open seven days a week in some area or another. Wednesday was 'Dancing Night', and Fridays and Saturdays were for Discos and Big Bands. Running at the same time was a cabaret from Wednesdays to Saturdays, and every night the restaurant was open for á la carte meals. Every other night the ballroom was filled with functions and weddings.

For four nights a week at the Glen we had Ron Williams and the Dixies performing. One of the main vocalists was Bonnie Tyler, one of the Dixies. I got to know her and her husband Bobbie Sullivan quite well. Bobby was an Olympic Judo Champion.

Bonnie, Bobby and Nicole.

64

On the top floor of the building was the Cave Cabaret Lounge which could hold 200 people. The artists who starred in the cabarets included Ryan and Ronnie, Emile Ford, Ruby Murray, Mac and Katie Kassoon, Craig Douglas, Mungo Jerry and many more.

Also on the top floor was the á la carte restaurant where our main chef was an Italian named Salvo. This restaurant would remain open late into the evening to accommodate the potential diners from the ballroom and cabaret. We would often enjoy a late meal in the restaurant with the main acts that were appearing that week. Amongst the many stars that appeared in the main ballroom were Slade, Amen Corner with Andy Fairweather Lowe, Marmalade, Leo Sayer, Screaming Lord Sutch, May Fisher, Helen Shapiro, David Bowie, Status Quo, Bad Finger and The Who and many others. The Who were the only band that completely wrecked our dressing room – they ended up smashing the windows and paying us a big compensation payment.

As we were paying so much money out to attract the big artists of the day, it was decided that if we opened an entertainment agency then we could book all the acts through the agency and at the same time gain the agency discount of 10%. The agency was called John Long Entertainments trading as 'Centa Artists' and our manager Peter Phillips ran it for us. We set up an office within the Glen and it worked successfully. At the same time we 'bankrolled' three rock groups, one of them was a wonderful group from Cardiff called 'Ingroville' and we supported them by supplying most of their equipment and a van, and we paid for a record to be released. After 18 months we ran out of patience with them and when we sold the Glen we closed the Entertainments Agency. Peter Phillips went to London to join another agency there –doing the same job in management.

Vince Eager (my friend from the 2i's days) also appeared at the Glen Ballroom. It was the first time that I had seen him in 15 years. He is seen here presenting me with his latest album with

Mike John, manager of the entertainment centre and Ian Scott, manager of the 10 pin bowling lanes.

Vince Eager presents me with his latest disc. Left is Mike John and right is Ian Scott.

Mike John, who was now my function director had had a few professional boxing fights in his younger days, and because of this experience he decided to apply for a licence to become a professional boxing promoter. During my stay at the Glen we held a number of professional 'Diner and Fight' nights. They were very well attended and on three occasions we had Eddie Thomas the boxing promoter ringside because at that time he was managing a Merthyr Boxing Stable and he came to support his boys.

When I had bought the Glen ballroom I had also bought a parcel of land behind the building. I made the mistake of not applying for outline planning and three years later the council put a compulsory purchase order on the land as they wanted to build a new council headquarters. They could not go ahead with

Vince Eager at the bowling alley.

their plans without my derelict land. After I dug my heels in, I managed to get two better offers and finally accepted £13,000 for the prime site. If I had had the foresight to apply for planning permission before the applied the C.P.O. then I would have expected to receive five times that amount!

I sold the Glen ballroom and bowling alley business in 1976 to young Dave Scott, (son of Dave Scott senior from whom I had purchased it six years earlier). He ran the entertainments business for a number of years eventually selling it to Terry Griffiths O.B.E. Terry now runs a very successful snooker hall, 'Terry Griffiths Matchroom' in the former ballroom.

Terry Griffiths Matchroom.

Terry Griffiths O.B.E. was born in Llanelli in 1947, and became world snooker Champion in 1979. After a successful career in which he won (amongst others) the Masters, Pot Black, U.K. Championship, the World Cup with the Wales team and Welsh Professional Championship, he announced his retirement in 1996, but played one last game at the Crucible in 1997 losing to Mark Williams in a final frame decider.

Terry is now a snooker coach and frequently commentates on snooker for B.B.C. television.

John Long with Terry Griffiths O.B.E. at the Terry Griffiths Matchroom, originally the Glen Ballroom. I later purchased the table on which Terry had won the World Championship in 1979.

Diversification had seemed the only way to go at that time. In hindsight I was working night and day and in the end something had to give. After two years of the extra business, things were deteriorating personally at home. There were daily rows between my in-laws and their son Huw which were reflecting on the business. I had made him, Les and Ann directors of my business and given them all shares in the company and when I made the difficult decision to leave home to sort myself out, the three directors got together and made my life untenable. I had given them collectively more shares than I had, so they ganged up on me and voted me off the board of my own company.

About the same time that I bought the Glen ballroom I started going out with my now wife Cheryl. I knew her to say 'hello' to for about a year because she worked as a secretary to a small oil company next to our building in Berthlwyd, Penclawdd. One summer's evening we went for a swim on a Gower beach together and everything started from there. After seeing each other for over two years discreetly, the split with my wife came and we moved in together. Since that date we have been together for over thirty five years and have spent the roller coaster days of business together.

During our Glen days, Cheryl and I often went to London shopping and on a few occasions Geoff Ash (my RAF mate) and his wife Viv would invite us to have dinner with them at Langan's. Geoff by this time was the sales manager of Olympus cameras. Langan's was the hottest restaurant in London in the seventies and was owned by two partners, Peter Langan and Sir Michael Caine. The restaurant was next door to the Mayfair Hotel and reservations had to be made weeks in advance – especially if you wanted to dine downstairs with all the celebrities. The partners always had table number 1, and Geoff had table number 2. He entertained his Olympus clients there by day and his friends most nights of the week.

Peter Langan was an eccentric Irishman who accepted paintings from impoverished artists in lieu of payment, and the walls of the restaurant were covered in works of art – including a Lucien Freud and a David Hockney. It became accepted in the restaurant that sometime late in the evening Peter Langan would wobble, fall on the floor and go to sleep in a drunken stupor. Customers became accustomed to stepping over the man in a white suit.

On one occasion on my way to the toilet I had to pass table number 1, where a drunken Peter Langan was holding court. He jumped up and staggered towards me and shook my hand saying, "Nice to see you again, Barry!" He then introduced me to his friends as 'the great Barry John!' I didn't dare correct him as he was notorious for abusing customers male or female. In latter years Peter Langan's actions became more and more erratic and one night in 1988, in a drunken daze after a fight with his wife, he set fire to his home and died of 70% burns.

Geoff Ash died in 1986 and I lost a good friend. Since that

time we have been to Langan's on a number of occasions with Viv where she is still treated as a special customer.

In 1972, we decided to buy a house in Palmyra Court in West Cross, Swansea. It was a brand new 2,800 sq. ft. house being built by Brian Cornelius who had six houses built facing his own super house. Haydn Williams from Old Walls, one of the finest stone masons in Gower, with the help of his son Keith built me a large fireplace out of Gower stone and a number of stone walls. The travelling to and fro to Llanelli really didn't suit us, so I sold the house to the new manager of Swansea City Football Club whose name was Harry Gregg. Harry was one of the survivors of the Munich air crash and he became famous because when everyone else was scrambling to get out of the wrecked aircraft, Harry went back in a number of times to pull out survivors. Harry played as goalkeeper for Manchester United and England and was probably the best goalkeeper of our time.

Cheryl was a motorbike fanatic in her early formative years and was a pillion passenger with a gang of bikers from the Gowerton area called The Eagles. One day they all descended on the Dolphin Inn, Llanrhidian 'en masse' in their leathers, but Mrs. Long took one look at them and decided that she just didn't need their business and refused them entry. It's funny that Mum took to Cheryl from the first time she met her with me, but we never ever told her of the biking incident!

Cheryl

71

Cheryl and I moved to a flat in Station Road, Llanelli and in October 1973 I took a lease in a 6,000 sq. ft. building in Sandy Bridge, Llanelli to start retailing again.

There were no refinements at Sandy Bridge such as running water, heating or toilet facilities. So to say that we roughed it was a fair assessment of our early days. Sales were made and then the goods were delivered by Brian and I – on one occasion at 10 p.m. to Newcastle Emlyn, made worse by the failure of the van to start, which was solved by pushing and bump starting it. My friend Vincent Jones, who had a wholesaling business in Skewen, gave me £5,000 worth of toys and fancy goods on the understanding that I would pay him back before Christmas Day. I actually paid him back just two weeks later, so we were back in the retailing business again. Between October and Christmas we did over £50,000 worth of business which seemed to be a good start at that time.

During the middle of 1973 I had my old friend Alexis Korner to do a show at the Glen. It was a sell out.

After the show we were having a meal together in our restaurant when I asked him to talk to his big buddy Mick Jagger

The Stones in concert.

72

to see if he would do a show for us at Pembroke Castle that summer. The Stones had just been turned down from appearing in Cardiff Castle and I thought that Pembroke would be just as good a location and I knew that they were very keen to do a castle venue.

I went to see the leader of Pembroke County Council who agreed that they would let us put a big show on there and the date Saturday, September 22nd was chosen as the big day. The management of The Stones came with me to meet the leader of the council and everything was finalised. It came out in the press, tickets were issued, extra trains from London were laid on, and then the bombshell burst. It seemed that because the councillors were in summer recess, the leader had taken it on his own back to agree to the show and now he was getting flak from some of the local councillors who were concerned with the Safety and Vandalism aspect.

The final straw came when he received a direct phone call from the President of CBS America who said that 'they were going to relay the show and scenes of Pembrokeshire coastline to every major city in America, every local hotel would be full, The Stones would arrive by helicopter etc. etc. and all at once the council leader realised the magnitude of his decision and after an emergency meeting with some of the objectors it was decided to 'pull' the show. So near and yet so far! The ticket price for the show with ten supporting acts was £2. 50 – not bad when you realise that they are charging £160 per ticket now in America for a similar line-up. So the local West Wales council lost the only chance to see the greatest band in the world, and also from having the biggest boost to the hotel and service industries free of charge. (They don't always get it right, do they?)

In the 1960s Alexis was credited with being the helping hand to the careers of the Rolling Stones, Led Zeppelin, Free, The Animals and many many more. His biggest hit was 'Tap turns on the water' which was produced by none other than Mickey Most from my 2 i's days! He went for a medical check after not feeling well and in 1983 he found he had cancer. He died on the 1st January 1984 at the age of 55. He was a wonderfully outgoing guy and there are still programmes about him and his 'blues' music on the radio today. He had a hide-away cottage in mid Wales where Cheryl and I visited him occasionally.

Chapter 5

MOVING ON

The Business Expands

Because my first wife and in-laws were using the title John Long Furnishers Ltd., I had to form a new company called John Long (West Wales) Ltd. From now on all our acquisitions would be made in that name. In 1974 we opened another shop in Llanelli selling mainly carpets with John Davies (JD) as manager. A year later we opened one in Milford Haven on the side of the docks. It was quite a large store under the management of Les and Dilys Perriam. Next came a store in Carmarthen under the management of Dilwyn and Mair Davies. From that moment on we were trading over £1 million per annum while at the same time the old regime in Gorseinon run by my in-laws was losing money at a terrible rate. In the four years between 1973 and 1977 their stock went from £250,000 down to £18,000. The inevitable happened. In December 1977 I bought the 75% shareholding from Ann, Les and Huw, otherwise the company would have folded. So the Gorseinon store was again in our fold and back where it belonged.

In March 1978, Gorseinon was trading profitably in its own right and within six months we were looking to more than double the size of the warehouse. In the next three years we put on three extensions, increasing the floor size from 10,000 sq. ft. to 43,000 sq ft. In 1983 a further 6,000 sq. ft. was added giving us a total of nearly 50,000 sq. ft. of selling space.

We celebrated with a 5 page spread in the Herald of Wales, in which we included photographs of our staff and acknowledged their contribution to the success of the store.

One of seven furniture bays inside the Gorseinon store.

Gorseinon store.

76

Newspaper cutting of staff.

In September 1976 Cheryl and I were married in Swansea Registry Office in front of six of our closest friends. It was very odd that the three girls had all bought their dresses without any knowledge of what anyone else was wearing, and they all had the same style dress as Cheryl but in different colours. David was a Director of Barclays Bank in the London area and he retired at the young age of 47. He was then head-hunted by Berkeley Homes PLC and he has now finally retired. Elaine was a registrar in Windsor and now they have returned to Landimore in Gower after 20 years away. We see them frequently.

Our wedding. From left –Dave & Elaine Martin, Hedley & Margaret, Cheryl & me, John & Nelda Jones.

The service went off well until the registrar asked me for payment for the cost of the ceremony and marriage certificate. I found that I didn't have any money on me at all and had to borrow it from the photographer. Come to think of it, I didn't pay him back! We held a small reception in Ashley's restaurant in Mumbles and went on honeymoon for a week. We didn't have time to spend any longer away because there was so much happening in our lives with the business.

Cheryl's Mum passed away with a brain haemorrhage in 1978. She was a wonderful person and took to me (and me to her) from the first time we met. She was only 57 years of age and was so close to Cheryl. The only comfort that we had was that Cheryl was in their farmhouse when it happened. She was rushed immediately by ambulance to Singleton Hospital but never recovered consciousness.

October 1977 started with us buying our house 'Warborough'. The house and land was bought from the bank by a consortium of six families. No one wanted our house because of its size and condition; they only wanted six plots from our garden, so that each one could build their own houses. They all did a fine job and we screened the houses behind tall Leylandii trees. We loved the house from the minute we saw it and immediately started extensive renovations.

We had in fact, prior to this, bought some land in Furnace with the intention of building our home there, but after falling in love with Warborough we sold the land off in five plots for £2,000 per plot. Coincidentally, Terry Griffiths lives on one of our plots at this time.

Warborough.

79

As the business grew, I was able to arrange surprise 'treats' for the family. The first being a weekend trip to Portmeirion with Cheryl and myself were Mum, Pat, Brian and his wife Dawn. The accommodation was superb and we would dress formally for dinner, and then meander our way through the gardens and around the goldfish pools to a luxurious meal in the restaurant. Another trip that was planned for the whole family was a mini cruise on the Q.E. 2, but Mum was unfortunately not well enough to travel and as Pat stayed home to care for her we asked my business friend Vince Jones and his wife Margaret if they would come instead, which they did and we all had a great time. On our last night on board we played Bingo and I won the £300 jackpot. This was shared out amongst the six of us. Within a month of the trip, Vincent died of a brain haemorrhage.

Between 1974 and 1977 our staff grew from just Cheryl and me, to include Brian, his wife Dawn and about twenty other personnel. To keep the family feeling going in the company we started taking all the staff on various holidays paid for by the company.

Capri holiday.
Included here are – John & Nora Davies, Ray & Kath Bush, Dewi Jones, Viv & Marie Howard, John & Nelda Jones, Dick & Bridget Lewis, Brian & Dawn Long, Jack & Pat Williams, John & Cheryl, Henry & Cath Jones.

We are shown here all flying off for a 5 day break in Capri. This followed our first year trip to Benidorm and our third year holiday took us to Majorca.

Majorca.
Included here are – Viv and Marie Howard, Brian and Dawn Long, Dilys and Les Periam, John and Nora Davies, Ray and Kath Bush, Dick and Bridget Lewis, Dewi Jones, Peter Sharpe, John and Nelda Jones, Kevin and Ann Bush.

These trips certainly helped the company to grow and everybody pulled together and undoubtedly put themselves out to help in anyway they could. As soon as we took over Gorseinon – on the 31st December 1977 – our staff numbers rocketed. At one time we had over one hundred personnel, and we could no longer afford the time or the cost of keeping the overseas trips going.

However, we did have some fantastic parties in the North Gower Hotel to try to make up for it.

I planned a surprise to celebrate Cheryl's 40thh birthday. I hired a private plane and two pilots to take us from Swansea Airport to Jersey. Hedley and Margaret Lewis, Nelda and John Jones came with us. Everybody had a surprise because they all thought that I had booked a weekend break in London. The pilot was Captain Oliver.

40th Birthday surprise with Hedley & Margaret Lewis, Nelda Jones, Cheryl, John Jones and me.

Over the years, I have always had numerous people asking me if I would like to invest in various projects and one project came to fruition when I heard that Llanelli Mercury Printing Company was going into liquidation. The company had been going for decades and their foreman had been with them all his life. He asked me if I would like to buy the assets of the company and set him up elsewhere, so I purchased all the printing presses and equipment and started 'Island Press' in John Street with Gwynfor as the

Columbian Press.

working boss. Five years later I gave Gwynfor all my shares and he successfully ran the company for over twenty five years. One of the interesting machines that Mercury had in the foyer was an 1837 Columbia Printing Press in excellent working condition. This was one of the few left in working complete condition in the whole country, because it is about 8ft. high and has a large cast Golden Eagle with spread wings on the top with twined snakes on the side frame. The feet were cast as claws. The unusual thing is that most of the eagles throughout the country were smashed off during the war years and the Third Reich period because they reminded people of the Hitler regime. This is now on loan to Swansea Museum.

In 1979 our contracts division had a big order to furnish and fit out 'Baskerville Hall Mansion'. (It had been used in the film 'The Hound of the Baskervilles'.) It had been taken over by a wealthy, Ferrari-driving youngster who had made his fortune by producing and selling garden gnomes and who was a millionaire by the age of 18! The name of the hotel was Clyro Court Hotel.

All the twelve bedrooms were themed (Chinese/Malay/ Egyptian etc.) and were all very extravagant and over the top and although every major retailer in South Wales was competing for the contract, we supplied a large of amount of carpets, beds, headboards etc. to the value of £4,000 –which was a good order in those days.

Unfortunately when we met the 'Gnome King' he was broke but he had such a front that everyone was taken in. Cheryl and I went to the hotel on two occasions to try to get some money out of him but he was too clever for us. On one occasion we booked a meal there and on arriving we were told that the chef was ill, so there would be no meals that night. The truth was that the chef had taken off because he was owed three months wages! We did in fact meet Lionel Bart there who was freeloading at the hotel and appeared to be on brandy morning, noon and night. (He owed so much money that he had just sold all the rights to 'Oliver!' and all his music to try to get himself out of trouble.) I asked him if he would like a drink with us and that cost me half a bottle of brandy!

I must tell you how the saga ended. Two weeks later, after getting a court order for our outstanding money, Cheryl and I were away on holiday when it was arranged that Brian would go to Clyro with the Sheriff of Brecon to put a levy on all our goods. He met the Sheriff at 7 am. in the car park of the Baskerville Arms (a local pub), and they drove at 70 miles an hour up the long winding drive to the hotel to surprise the occupants.

This wasn't the first visit for the Sheriff because he had been there on another occasion to collect £10,000 for a large store in Cardiff that had supplied some sumptuous bedroom furniture. After banging on the door of the Chinese Room, the door was opened by an irate client in bathrobes who asked him what he thought he was doing. On hearing that the Sheriff was taking all the furniture to service some of the debt the coloured occupant asked how much the debt was and on being told the amount, he gave the Sheriff a cheque for the £10,000 sum because he wanted to be left alone with his lady friend. It turned out that the occupant was the Prince of Tonga and the cheque was a good one!

All our goods had already been taken away by some other persons, but we did, much to their annoyance, clear all the staff quarters of beds, wardrobes, etc., which we put into auction in Cardiff. We eventually lost about £3,000.

January 1980 was a very memorable month for us. We had just finished a 20,000 sq. ft. extension and before we started moving furniture in we had a call from a loss adjuster in Birmingham to say that he had a very large insurance claim and they wanted to shift over £½ million pounds worth of furniture (35 containers full) to anyone who could take it all in one go. As luck would have it, we had the space and the money to take it all and we opened the new extension with the best event in our history. It really was The Sale of the Century –we took £100,000 in one day!

Western Mail advertisement 1980.

We are seen here celebrating the completion of the largest single order for our contracts division. Vivian Howard (centre) with the help of Dave Williams (on my left) managed to win the order for the complete refurbishment of 1,000 bedrooms for all the employees working on the new oil refinery in Milford Haven. This was a mammoth task to organise but with all our hands on deck we completed the supply and fit out of 1,000 beds, wardrobes, chests of drawers, bedside chests and lamps, head boards, floor rugs etc. on time. Not long after this time, Eddie Morgan (on Brian's right) collapsed and died in the office.

Eddie was a wonderful man. He was a qualified pilot (he took me flying many times) and he flew with Lancaster Bombers in the war. He was present at the bombing of Cologne in Germany and told me that they had been instructed not to bomb Cologne Cathedral, so that was left standing amongst the complete devastation all around.

This poem of Eddie's had been written by him in copperplate lettering. It was read at his funeral.

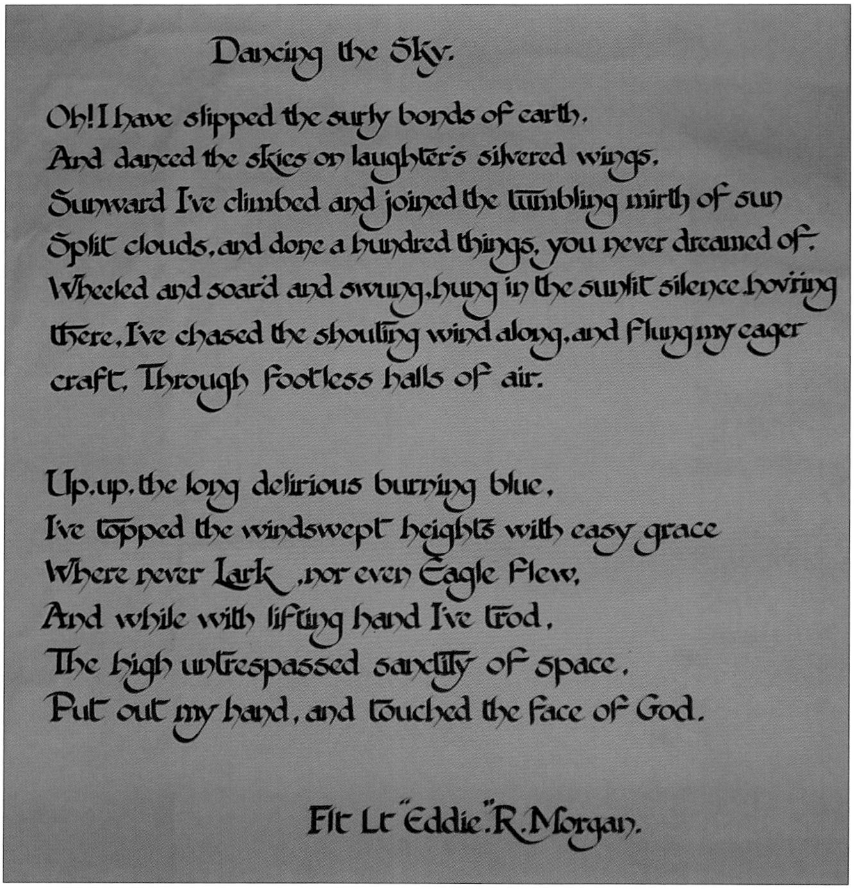

Dancing the Sky.

Oh! I have slipped the surly bonds of earth,
And danced the skies on laughter's silvered wings.
Sunward I've climbed and joined the tumbling mirth of sun
Split clouds, and done a hundred things, you never dreamed of,
Wheeled and soar'd and swung, hung in the sunlit silence, hovering
there, I've chased the shouting wind along, and flung my eager
craft, Through footless halls of air.

Up, up, the long delirious burning blue,
I've topped the windswept heights with easy grace
Where never Lark, nor even Eagle Flew,
And while with lifting hand I've trod,
The high untrespassed sanctity of space,
Put out my hand, and touched the face of God.

Flt Lt "Eddie" R. Morgan.

After Eddie died we advertised for a replacement Financial Director to take his place. Out of a number of applicants we finally chose Peter Woolard who was very able and fitted in with us right away. Peter stayed with us until I sold the business in 1985. We are still friends today.

In April 1982 we sponsored the 'Ras de Cymru' Round Wales Cycle Race for the leg between Gorseinon and Aberystwyth. This picture shows me 'Flagging them off' with our J/L logo flag, with some of our staff cheering them on!

Ras de Cymru

I had a call from an Insurance Loss Adjuster saying that there had been a terrible fire at the Co-op in Weston super Mare and would I be interested in tendering for the entire stock of the store. I went down to Weston to have a look at it and was shocked to see that the whole store was totally smoke damaged. Everything was black! The suites, china, rugs, cutlery, clothing, shoes, bedroom furniture – everything! I put a bid in for the whole stock including the wines, spirits and tins of baked beans etc. and finally got the job.

As everything was covered in smoke we had to wash every item and had a team of girls (including my mother, Pat, my daughter Sian, Dawn (Brian's wife) and several friends to wash and dry everything, and we advertised a bumper sale. This is no exaggeration – the queue outside our Gorseinon Warehouse stretched six deep from the front of our building nearly down to Gorseinon. We had security on the front doors allowing ten people in and ten out at one time all day long for three days. It was great to see all the action and we had three cash points throughout the store. There was one downside to all this cash piling in because we caught one of our staff pinching £500. We called the police and after a three hour grilling she finally confessed, and we got the £500 bundle back. The most hurtful part of this was that she was a lay-preacher and this wasn't the first time that she had done this to us.

You can't go on face value any more!

Later in 1982 we were involved in the purchase of 18 Sherman Tanks from Portugal. All were used in the 1940s routing of Rommel in the Middle East. The one that I selected for us had eighty miles registered on the mileometer, and it still had sand inside the body. We placed the tank outside the showroom window, and hundreds of people were taking photographs on or in front of it. In 1984 we took over a very large building outside Caerphilly on a lease and to help promote it we had an old Rolls Royce and a Sherman tank on display inside the showroom. Its funny, but people always remember us for the gimmicks and not the service and price. The tank was still drivable after all these years and not only did John Jones drive it but I had a go on the land behind our Gorseinon depot.

John Long and tank.

Army cadets and tank.

At this time, we also had a very large premises (30,000 sq. ft.) situated on The Point in Penclawdd, where regular imports of contract furniture were stored, together with a variety of salvage items for sorting and sometimes cleaning. Both of these occupied approximately one third of the warehouse space so there was plenty of room for additional income, which after careful brokering, was solved by doing a deal with the Milk Marketing Board to store Skimmed Milk Powder in uniform stocks of 40 ton batches readily available for call off at 24 hours notice. The containers started arriving at any time between 7 am. and 7 pm. from the Whitland or Felinfach Creameries and were 'hand balled' into the 40 ton stacks until we finally had 2,000 tons in storage ready for their call off as and when required, but most importantly the rental from the M.M.B. meant that there was no depreciation in the value of our normal regular stocks of furniture. Milk powder continued to be stored there for more than two years, until the Gorseinon business was leased to Waring and Gillow. By this time all the milk powder had been sold off to the continent for animal feed. For a while, Brian ran this side of the business very successfully.

My daughter Sian with Cheryl amongst the milk powder storage.

In 1983 we entered a Window Dressing Competition promoted by the British Wool Council and a Midlands Suite manufacturer and out of every participating store in Britain we were the winners. The prize was a holiday for two people, all expenses paid, to Australia. The idea was put together by one of our nicest staff members – Steve, so we offered him the prize. He turned it down so Cheryl and I went in his place and in Australia we met up with my pal Spike from the RAF and his wife Dee.

Not very long after this time, Steve didn't turn up for work one Monday morning. He had gone missing while walking his dog on the cliffs in Gower. All the staff went down to the coast to look for him but to no avail. His body was recovered from the sea a week or so later. Evidently he had had financial problems and that may have been the cause of him walking in to the sea. If we had been told of his problems I'm sure that we would have helped in any way we could, because he was such a good salesman and was liked by the customers and staff alike. We all went to his funeral and closed the shop that day as a mark of respect to him.

With 'John Long's, West Wales Ltd.' being given access to many licensed premises throughout Wales and England, with our 'made to measure' bench seating and bar furniture together with soft furnishings, it made sense when the opportunity arose, to purchase an automatics company involving a thousand plus pool tables, juke boxes and one arm bandits. In 1984, I heard that Booths of Tenby were contemplating selling their fruit machine rental business. It wasn't on the market but one of their managers dropped the hint that they could be persuaded to sell. I contacted them and after lengthy discussions I bought their premises in Tenby and Paignton (Devon), and over one thousand sited fruit machines and pool tables all over South Wales and South Devon. We called it 'John Long Automatics'. The purchase of this company increased the strength and variety of the contracts division and offered complete package deals to existing and new customers which necessitated opening up a showroom and depot in Paignton. However, I found it a difficult business to handle and after 18 months I sold the whole business, lock, stock and barrel to Buckley's Breweries because it suited them to own a company that could also supply their own eighty or so pubs in South Wales with a constant supply of fruit machines and pool tables.

We leased the store in Caerphilly with the proviso that the landlords repaired the roof. We moved in at great expense and started trading there very successfully until the local council put a stop notice on us for selling toys and Christmas fancy goods on a sizeable portion of the 100,000 sq. ft. store.

Caerphilly store.

After three months the flat roof was leaking all over the place and the owners, after promising us that they were going to fix the problem told us that they were in financial difficulty and couldn't afford the £100,000 – £150,000 that may be needed to get the flat roof repaired.

This, coupled with the council problem put me on such a downer that I decided to cut our losses and pull out of Caerphilly. In hindsight I should have bought the site myself. It's easy to be wise after the event!

1985 started with a dreadful catastrophe. On the first Tuesday in January I was supposed to go to the Bankers' Dinner in Swansea University as a guest of the Bank with one of my best friends Vincent Jones. That morning we had a telephone call to say that Vincent had been rushed into hospital with a brain haemorrhage. We thought that as he was only 37 he was bound to recover. I went to the Bankers' Dinner on my own and came from the bash early to go to sit with Cheryl and Vince's wife Margaret and kids all night. Vincent died the following day, and I can still feel the pain because not only did he get me started again in 1973, but we did everything together – holidays, nights out – and only two days before he died we put a plan together to merge both our very successful businesses and go public.

Vincent's death changed things so much. I made a decision to get out of my pride and joy warehouse in Gorseinon. After six months of negotiations I finally leased the whole building to a new company called G.P. Homestore who was quickly taken over by Waring and Gillow – a big public company that wanted to expand retailing into West Glamorgan. They paid me a rental of £52,000 p.a., with a large rent review to come on the first review date.

After leaving Gorseinon we opened an office in our Sandy Bridge Warehouse and stayed to run our mini empire from there. In the early 90s we built a new warehouse for our club and pub import business and built some better office accommodation and we are still there in that building today.

Chapter 6

FAMILY AND FRIENDS

Mum

Mum with her family.
Back row – Brian, Pat and John, seated, from left – Helen, Sian, Mum, Thomas, Cheryl and Dawn.

Mum was born Lily May Howells in Brynhyfryd, Swansea in 1909. When she was about 15, she went to work as a cook's assistant in Llwyn Derw Mansion, West Cross for the Folland family. The house later became an annexe for Swansea Hospital.

Llwyn Derw Mansion at the time of the Folland family.
By kind permission of Gower author Mrs. Anne Roberts.

It is very strange, but 55 years later I bought the house not knowing of any earlier connection. She met Dad and later, when he was offered a job as a green keeper in London, they became engaged and she followed him to London. Finally Dad had a job back in the Swansea area as a golf professional, so they returned to Fairways, Armine Road. They then moved to 19, Armine Road, where I was born five years later.

After 21 years in the Dolphin, Mum wanted to retire. She knew that Mr. Winch was selling his house Homeside at auction. Mr Winch was a well known village character and his wife Beatrice had run the local post office. He was the church organist at Llanrhidian Church for many years in spite of his blindness. Mum very astutely asked her accountant to attend the auction and bid on her behalf. He frightened the other bidders off with his aggressive style of bidding and bought it for Mum. After making some alterations, Mum left the hard years at the Dolphin behind and retired with Pat to Homeside.

Around 1973, Mum decided to leave the village and moved to Brynmill, Swansea and that is where she died in 1987.

Everyone will say that their mother was the best, but I can honestly say that she looked after us on her own, and brought us

96

all up to be a credit to her. Without her financial help in the beginning I am certain that I could never have survived. I was most grateful and paid her back with interest.

Cheryl's father died on the 27th March, 1986 aged 78, after farming all his life. He owned a farm in Waunarlwydd that happened to be on the fringe of a housing development, and in the early 1970s he sold some land to Brian Cornelius, a local Swansea developer, for a large amount of money. Firstly he did the farm up to have a few home comforts that had been missing in his life for years, and then he bought himself a Jensen Interceptor and later a Rolls Royce, (but took the mascot off the front because it would look too ostentatious to the people around him in Waunarlwydd). He didn't want to know me until Cheryl's mother died and after that we got on well together and many times I would pick him up in my 'roller' and take him for a trip around Gower. Towards the end of his life he even allowed me to drive him in his Rolls Royce – that was quite something because he really loved and took care of his cars.

After he died, the family sold his Rolls Royce but kept his mascot on a stand in our lounge.

Sian

My daughter Sian was born in December 1966. It had taken eight years to happen and she was thoroughly spoiled by everyone. She was a very contented child and I was so proud that she was mine. Six years later her mother and I split up, and there were many problems with me seeing her. Even though I wanted to see her on a regular basis, it was so much easier for the child not to be pulled from pillar to post and so I didn't officially see her until she was about 15, when she came to help, of her own accord, in the Gorseinon Warehouse to earn some money for herself. I supported her when she went to a modelling school in London where she met her first husband Sardi. She is a beautiful girl and I am sure that with luck she would have been **someone** in the London modelling scene.

Sian in her modelling days.

They then came home to Swansea to get married and sometime later her mother was taken ill and finally died of cancer. I regret not going to her wedding and also not seeing my first wife before the end, but every break-up is difficult and never ends the way it should. Sian and Sardi had two beautiful daughters Yasmin and Amber.

Finally in 1990 Sian and I got back together and since then we have been very close. I love her dearly.

After Sian's marriage broke up, she started seeing Jonathan Hale Quant. At that time he was running the Penyscynor Bird and Animal Park in Neath with the help of his mother Jackie Quant. The park had been started in the 1960s by Jonathan's grandfather Idris Hale, a renowned builder in South Wales. Jonathan had been brought up in Penyscynor and over the years there was a steady decline in the attendance figures and it was decided to close the park and sell off the land to a large P.L.C.

After the sell-off, Jonathan decided to go into the building business himself and formed a company called Baytree Homes with John Rewbridge a fellow director and my daughter Sian as company secretary. Over the last five years they have built quite a number of quality homes and at present have sites in Neath and Llanelli on the go.

Sian 2nd left with friends.

Sian.

When Sian and Jonathan married on the 18th May 2002, we held their wedding reception for 140 people in the Ashburnham Hotel. With their daughter Isabelle we now have three beautiful granddaughters. I am so pleased to see Sian settled with her own loving family and Jonathan's extended family is a close comfort. I am delighted to see that Jonathan has all the entrepreneurial enthusiasm that I had at his age, and it looks as if some of my passion has been passed on to Sian, who apart from her clerical work with Baytree, enjoys co-ordinating colour schemes and furnishing their show house interiors.

Yasmin, Isabelle and Amber.

Front row from left – Yasmin, Amber, Isabelle, Sian and Johnathan.

Yasmin is bright, athletic and ambitious and has reached an age where she has to decide in which direction her future lies. Not an easy time, but we have all had to make choices and take our chances, and I am sure that she will choose wisely. Amber is sensitive, artistic and determined and is just starting out on that important school path of examinations. Isabelle is a beautiful, bubbly young girl and like so many of her age loves to entertain. They are all so individual and it is such a pleasure to watch them grow. I wish you health and a lot of happiness, girls.

Pat

From left – Cheryl, Pat, Dawn and Brian.

My sister Pat is one of the kindest people I know. She will help anyone and even though she doesn't have much money she will contribute to all causes and tries to help in any possible way.

When Mum died Pat told Brian and I that she wanted to go back to the village to live. We searched all the possible houses that were available at the time and it was six months later that we had the good fortune to find "Three Ways" on the market, right next door to the Dolphin. It is in the heart of the village and that is where Pat has lived contentedly over the last 17 years. If there is a trip going somewhere, a meeting of the Senior Citizens or the Mothers' Union, Pat is always present.

On the other hand, the locals really look after her and always include her when they go somewhere. You cannot have better neighbours than Margaret (The Dolphin), Dick and Edna Beynon, Dora, young Mike (Dolphin) and Martin (Big House). All these and many more have helped her in so many ways. We are grateful and will never forget your kindness.

Brian

Brian and Dawn celebrating Christmas with us.

My brother Brian retired from working with us as a company director in March 1993. He was certainly my right hand man and was someone I could rely and depend on completely over the years. He accepted the fact that I might divert from one business to another and in all our thirty years in business together we never had a cross word. He is the only person that I know who, when alone in the showroom sold a three piece suite to customers, whilst lying flat out on the floor unable to move his head because of a Meniere's attack.

Brian and Dawn on holiday in Majorca after Brian's retirement.

And we are still very close today.

Nicole

We first met Nicole when we were advised by Terry Francis that if we ever were in San Francisco we were to telephone her number and she would show us all the sights of 'Frisco. We had, on this trip, been to New York, Washington and Las Vegas and ended up the trip in San Francisco, and by that time we were doubtful if we would bother to give her a call. Thank goodness we did! She spent four days taking us everywhere and explaining the sights – Top of the Mark, Telegraph Hill, China Town, Alcatraz and Fisherman's Wharf – and from that moment a great friendship was formed.

She came to the U.K. the following year and stayed with Cheryl and me for about three months before returning to San Francisco. During that time we learned all about her and her family.

Her grandfather was the founder member of Monsanto Chemicals (one of the largest chemical companies in the world). Her mother married a number of times. Nicole had two sisters

Nicole during her stay with us.

Nicole with Bill Walsh
(centre) and two officials.

With the security police at the game – Nicole 5th left, Cheryl 1st left, my daughter Sian 1st right with husband Sardi.

and they were all the offspring of their mother's marriage to a Frenchman. Nicole's mother lived on a very generous allowance all her life that meant that she had a fabulous house with a pool and staff quarters in the garden, lifts and a large staff of maids, gardeners etc. She spent all her days following Elvis Presley wherever he was appearing. She always had front row seats and was very friendly with Colonel Tom Parker and indeed Elvis himself. When her father (Nicole's grandfather) died, all the money was left in trust to Nicole and her two sisters.

When Nicole returned to San Francisco she felt that she had to do something so she got a job as Personal Assistant to Bill Walsh, the head coach of the San Francisco 49ers. (GOD!). He was the biggest coach in the history of the 49ers.

In fact, after they had won the Superbowl in 1989, they came to play at Wembley and we were invited to sit in the best seats in the house to watch the game.

Nicole invited Cheryl and I to stay with her as her guests in her sumptuous £2,000 per night apartment in Mayfair, London. It had three bedrooms, five bathrooms, a large gorgeous dining room, a sauna, 9 televisions and a kitchen, and came complete with a maid and butler. After breakfast was served, she decided that the three of us would go to purchase an 'itsy bitsy sweater' in Harrods. We made for the cashmere room and within two minutes she had six members of Harrods sale staff at her beck and call, and five minutes later she had spent over £20,000 on cashmere sweaters, dresses, and half a dozen pairs of £200 cashmere slippers. I ended up carrying the bulk of her purchases!

Dr. Hook

Dr. Hook with me.

Cheryl and I were driving along one day listening to the car radio playing a Dr. Hook song called 'Sylvia's mother' when I said 'If there is one special band that I must see in our lifetime then it must be Dr. Hook!' On returning to the office, Cheryl contacted the Radio Two programme who passed her on to the record company, who in turn passed her on to Dr. Hook's management company in Miami, Florida. U.S.A. They informed her that the band was, in fact, going to appear in Lahr, Germany on the 7th September 1996. They would be top of the bill with Suzie Quatro, Alvin Stardust and Hot Chocolate and they gave Cheryl the organisers' telephone number in Germany.

The whole show was organised by a local radio station 'Süd West Funk' and Cheryl spoke to the presenter of the show whose name was Vomey Schmit, (the German equivalent of Terry Wogan). He invited Cheryl and I and Patrick and Jeanette to be his guests at the concert and told her to ask for him at the entrance gates on arrival.

Because we had travelled such a distance, it was obvious that we were Big Fans of the band so Vomey interviewed us live on the radio station and invited us to meet Dr. Hook and his band after he had finished his set. We met Ray (Dr. Hook), his son K.C., and the whole band and had a great time with them and that was the start of a great friendship.

Since that time we have been guests of his at many shows around the country – Birmingham, Paignton, Wembley, and Bristol – we even got him to play one night to a sell-out crowd at the Grand Theatre in Swansea. On that night we picked the band up in the stretch limo and Ray and K.C. in the 'roller' to take them from the hotel to the Grand.

Because we had front row seats, during one of his songs Ray came off stage and sat on Patrick's lap singing a song to the four of us much to our delight and the enjoyment of the audience! After the performance we went back to the hotel with Ray and the band, and a great time was had by all until the early hours. For such a great star, he gave us a lot of his time. On the 2nd November 1997 we stayed with him at the Lakeside Country Club and Hotel in South London.

Ray, (wearing a jacket of mine that he had taken a fancy to) with Patrick, Cheryl and me overlooking the Lake.

Cheryl, Ray and Jeanette.

Chapter 7

BACK TO BUSINESS

February 1987 started rather strangely. We had just finished the January sales and Cheryl and I decided to go to the Carnival in Rio. We stayed at a superb hotel on Copacabana beach front and the weather was fabulous. The carnival procession stretched for miles, with elaborate floats and amazing costumes. It ended up in a large stadium area where there were about half a million people. We arrived there about 4 o'clock and stood amongst the huge crowd, and after about an hour I spotted two people from Llanelli pushing their way through the throng and heading in our direction.

Clive Hughes and his wife were on a Round the World trip and had also decided to stop over in Rio for the Carnival. Clive owns the large unit in the next yard to us in Sandy Bridge, and it was an incredible coincidence that halfway around the world, in the middle of the biggest crowd I had ever seen I would meet up with someone situated 50 yards from us in Llanelli! Clive now has a big construction business in Australia.

In 1988 I was offered the freehold of our Sandy Bridge site for £200,000 and bought it before the landlords had a chance to auction it off. This seemed a good deal to me as it included the tyre depot fronting the road, our 12,000 sq. ft. warehouse and three further warehouses and some land.

Early in 1989 I had a phone call from Patrick who was the manager of Waring and Gillow at their store warehouse in Gorseinon. Evidently the company wanted to get out of retailing everywhere west of Bristol and had offered him an extremely good deal if he would take the commitment of the 21 year lease left on the warehouse off their hands. To get this assigned, they had to have my permission as landlord. Of course, I agreed because I knew that Patrick was a good and conscientious manager for them. He had worked for me prior to Waring and Gillow so I knew how trustworthy he was. Because it was a big step to take at that time, Patrick asked me if I would go in with him in the venture, so I arranged the finance with our friendly bank manager and we joined forces. It has been a happy relationship ever since.

Jeanette and Patrick at Homestores.

Patrick is an extremely able company director and a good friend. We formed a limited company with Patrick and I joint directors and since that time Patrick has made the decisions and run the whole show with his wife Jeanette, and it is going from strength to strength. It is now another multi-million pound company and I'm proud to be part of it, thanks to both of them.

Also in 1989 I did an electrical salvage deal with Curry's. Although a fire had damaged only an outside office, £500,000 stock had to go because there was a hint of smoke in the

The interior of Homestores with Jeanette and Patrick.

large warehouse and showroom. I rented another warehouse in Fforestfach from Marshall David and we set out the goods inside.

A small portion of the Curry's salvage deal.

For security we put a night watchman on duty and locked him in the premises overnight. On the second night there was a break-in and when our security man challenged one of the intruders he had a television set thrown at him. He phoned for the police, who arrived two minutes later, but even though two of the intruders were still on the roof they failed to catch them. In spite of the fact that one of them landed awkwardly and damaged his leg they still got away!

Every large electrical deal meant that we had to put one or two night watchmen inside the buildings for safety's sake. Later on we had a break-in on the same site in Fforestfach and the robbers got away with a 40 ft. container lorry full of three piece suites. They were never recovered.

During this time the IRA left an incendiary device under the cushion of a 3 piece suite in one of the furniture departments in Harrods, Knightsbridge, London. After it had detonated, the subsequent blast meant that not only did the furniture in that department have to be cleared out to their repository by the side of the Thames, but also their book section which was the next department. We tendered for it all and got the lot! Much to our surprise, 98% of the stock was in perfect condition and because of its high quality sold very quickly. As well as furniture, the books were included in the insurance deal – amongst them were 50 leather bound First Edition books by various authors, which had a price tag of £300 or more. We sold all the books to a bookshop in Carmarthen but kept the First Editions.

Marshall David was the landlord of the units that I rented in Fforestfach, Swansea and also a close friend. Marshall told me that he was building minibuses in his own factory in the North of England, and lately, because it was an all day drive to the factory, he had been flying from Fairwood Airport in a local twin engine light aeroplane. This took the stress out of travelling and could be done in one day. I said that I had occasionally also

Marshall David.

112

used light aircraft (and still do as our base player in the band Kenny Evans has his own single engine plane which we use periodically). Marshall was adamant that under no circumstances was I ever to go up in a single engine plane!

He invited me to join colleagues on a flight to his factory, but on the day, as there were already three passengers, it was decided that I would travel on a later occasion. On the way back from the factory the **single** engined plane crashed in North Wales. Along with Marshall David were Ted Morgan, bank manager, and David Jenkins, who were killed instantly. I lost a few good friends that day, and was extremely lucky not to be with them.

In 1990 I was approached by accountant Colin Thomas and asked if I would like to take a share in the purchase of The Ashburnham Hotel, a run-down establishment in Pembrey, Llanelli.

The hotel has quite a place in history. It was built in 1823 by a London solicitor named Thomas Gaunt, who came to Pembrey as the superintendent of the iron works in Burry Port. In 1928 Amelia Earhart, the first woman to fly across the Atlantic Ocean, had spent her first night in Europe at the Ashburnham.

The Ashburnham Hotel in the early 20th century.

She had been invited to be a passenger on the transatlantic crossing of the sea plane 'Friendship' which was flown by Wilmer Stulz and Louis Gordon. The 'Friendship' took off from Trepassey in Newfoundland and landed in Burry Port twenty-one hours 40 minutes later. The plane was heading for Southampton but with fuel running low it landed in the Burry inlet.

Amelia Earhart.

I recommended the purchase of the hotel to my solicitor friend Bob Evans and it was decided that the three of us would buy it as a company and become the company's directors. As it was in such a bad state of repair our intention was to sell some of the 8 acres of land for building and to put the proceeds towards the complete renovation of the hotel. I spoke directly to two of the councillors concerned and they completely supported the idea as the hotel was an eyesore.

The Ashburnham before renovation.

The chief of planning at the council also supported the plan 100%, and on the strength of these meetings we purchased the hotel. We applied to the council formally and had the shock of our lives when at the local council meeting the councillors went against what was said privately and we were now left with a hotel that was near derelict, a hotel that needed £500,000 spent to upgrade and now no chance to raise the capital required to complete the upgrade from the sale of the land. After many nights of meetings we decided to 'bite the bullet'. We borrowed the extra money needed from a friendly bank manager Colin Cornelius, and did a wonderful job of refurbishment and opened the hotel to the public in July 1991. I supplied the hotel with furniture and carpets.

The Ashburnham today.

The first four years were difficult because the three of us were business men in our own field but not hoteliers. Gradually, with the help of our wives in various areas, things began to develop slowly. After getting rid of numerous male and female managers,

Colin Thomas's wife Sue took over the everyday running of the hotel. Bob Evans's wife Jennifer was responsible for the landscaping of the garden and grounds and Cheryl was in charge of all the refurbishing and colour schemes etc. All have done a wonderful job and without them we wouldn't be in the position that we are in today.

About six years ago, I called down to The Ashburnham only to be confronted by a number of armed plain clothes police officers in the building. It turned out that the Rev. Ian Paisley was staying at the hotel along with his retinue of Irish armed police, and a number of local policemen, all there for his protection. All very hush- hush! A bedroom was used as an arsenal for all the guns and ammunition that each officer had brought, and there was 24 hour security for the Reverend.

Rev. Paisley, who was much nicer to talk to than he was portrayed on television, was in the Llanelli area to officially open and preach at a new church in the area. Another first for The Ash! There is talk at this moment that on his retirement as First Minister of Northern Ireland, he will be awarded the Nobel Peace prize – we will wait and see!

The conservatory lounge bar.

The hotel is in a beautiful setting as it overlooks the championship Ashburnham golf links and is on the edge of the Millennium Coastal path. Nearby Burry Port has a picturesque harbour, and today The Ashburnham is one of the principal hotels in the area, and as it is registered for civil weddings many wedding celebrations are held there.

Sue and Colin Thomas.

The next venture to capture our attention was Benjamin Howells, a timber and sawmills company which had operated at a 5 acre site in New Dock, Llanelli since 1837, was taken over in mid 1970 by Reeves, Builders Merchants who subsequently put the site on the market for sale in 1992. Cheryl and I saw the 'For Sale' notice on the gates and we asked the Cardiff agents for a viewing. We liked the site so much that I travelled to the Cardiff office the following day. I gave them a 10% deposit cheque to make sure that I was going to have it at the asking price and left it to the solicitors to handle the exchange as soon as possible.

Two weeks later I was asked by the agents if I wanted to sell the site on for a profit of £20,000. I refused the offer because I really wanted the location to start a small industrial site there using all the existing buildings. I found out later that I had beaten the local council to the sale and they wanted it to make some essential road widening and straightening scheme. I subsequently did a deal with the council by allowing them ½ acre of the frontage for the same amount that I had paid for the whole site.

Three years later on when I wanted to erect another building on some of the land as I had filled all the existing units with tenants and needed more warehousing space, the council, because it suited them, would not grant me permission. In fact, they warned me that even though it had been industrial for over 150 years, they had now earmarked the site as a residential zone. Over the next year I moved the tenants on and later the building group B. J. did a joint venture with me and built 36 houses on the land. I was sorry to and disappointed to see the land go in the way that it did.

In 1993 Patrick from Homestores and I bought a nice large shop that used to be the Co-op in Skewen. For the first three or four years it was run as a bedding shop called Homestore Bedding and it was run mainly by Patrick's wife Jeanette. It was certainly the best property and site in Skewen and was a nice addition to the Homestore portfolio. This has now been leased out to another bedding shop and it seems to be doing extremely well.

1993 was a most memorable year. Patrick and I with our wives Janet and Cheryl went to America to visit 'Highpoint Furniture Show' in North Carolina. This is one of the biggest shows in the world. Highpoint is a furniture manufacturing city and everybody seems to work in the industry. Our intention in visiting Highpoint was to find a rocking chair that we could import from America with the intention of wholesaling them around Great Britain and Ireland. After three days we were disappointed because we couldn't find exactly what we wanted. In fact everything seemed to be made in Malaysia or China. One stand did catch our eye though.

We called in at a stand called 'Banker and Brisebois

Advertising' and were completely 'knocked out' by the innovation of their ideas and artwork which did not exist in the UK at that time. We called back to the stand on a number of occasions and realised that this product was the best that we had seen in a long time, and after lengthy negotiations Patrick bought the subscription service for Homestore's use in the UK.

Two months later, Patrick started using the service in his local advertising and very soon our competitors were congratulating us on the quality of the adverts and the 'punchy' messages that came from using them. Pretty soon the local papers were asking us who was doing our adverts and it was suggested that maybe we could supply the source to all the newspaper divisions in their group around the country.

We had to work fast because we were allowed to use the service for our own use only, so with the prospect of supplying everyone in Britain we all went back out to see Banker & Brisebois at their offices in Detroit, with the sole intention of buying the rights for the whole of the UK and Europe.

After three days of negotiations the meeting was joined by another of their advisers who really took a shine to us. It turned out that his mother and father came from, as he said – "You won't know this small village in Wales. It's called Hendy, Pontardulais". He had a shock when Patrick said that he was from Hendy, and from that moment on he was on our side and we purchased the rights to all their products and services for the whole of Britain, Ireland and Europe.

As we had very large offices above our Skewen branch we decided to form another company with Patrick and I as the principal shareholders. Hence Banker and Brisebois Ltd. came into being, and we started selling the advertising ideas mainly aimed at the furniture industry in the January Furniture Show in Birmingham, 1994. We took on Brian Cox (who was originally with the South Wales Evening Post) to handle all the changes that had to be made to get rid of all the 'Americanisms' from the adverts and he ran the complete show very successfully indeed.

119

Brian Cox with me in our office of Banker and Brisebois Advertising.

The Furniture Show in Birmingham was a brilliant success because the British retailers had not seen anything like our advertisements in the country before, and for the next three years we did amazing business.

Patrick and me at a trade fair.

Banker and Brisebois advertisements

Our downfall was that every month we gave too many advert ideas and over a period people started not to renew their next year's subscription because they already had such a selection and quantity sent to them that they had a backlog of ideas. We are, at present, negotiating with a large P.L.C. to allow them to have the rights to the U.K. on a percentage basis.

Pre Christmas
advertisement

In 1994, Patrick's store was bursting at the seams and he desperately needed some extra storage areas so he started renting a property in Queen's Avenue, Gorseinon. After renting for a year we finally bought the freehold. The same year we both went to Kuala Lumpur, Malaysia to purchase some rocking chairs that we had spotted in America.

After some lengthy negotiations we brought 2,000 of them in a K.D. form. We formed another company to import and assemble them under the name of 'Woodmasters Ltd.' and we used the Queen's Ave. property for that purpose. We had a number of agents spread over the country to sell these rockers and for a few years we had great success with them.

This was the sample on which we based our 'Woodmasters' rocker. After two years we sold all our stock and decided to move on. Furniture is a fashion industry!

1999 started extremely well. On one of my many trips down to visit our store in Milford Haven I noticed a large 'For Sale' sign in a property in Pensarn, Carmarthen. This property had been one of twenty sites around

Woodmaster chair.

the country that had been owned by a company called Kemira who are the biggest distributors of Agricultural fertilisers in the country. They were changing their distribution pattern and had made a board decision to sell all their depots around the country and deliver straight from their main factory in England. Hence Pensarn was surplus to requirements.

The 4½ acre site had two large units, both in a separate compound and they were asking £500,000 for the complete site. After speaking to the Cardiff agents I took Cheryl down to have a viewing. We were both very impressed with the potential of the site and placed a 10% deposit immediately to secure the deal. While we were awaiting completion we applied to Carmarthen County Council for a change of use and after three months we were permitted to change from warehousing to retailing, at the same time leaving the smaller 17,000 sq. ft. building as warehousing and storage. The large building measured 40,000 sq. ft.

In a short space of time we were able to rent out both properties to a local haulage and storage contractor. After a year in occupation the tenant persuaded me to sell the larger building to him and ever since he is still the tenant with use of the 17,000 sq. ft. building which remains in our portfolio.

The interior of the large unit at Pensarn before purchase.

Sometime in the 1990s, we had a call from the loss adjusters regarding an interesting insurance claim. It turned out that a 40 ft. container had been loaded with 2,000 boxed video recorder players at a well known 'brand' factory in Port Talbot, and was bound for a large Spanish retail chain when the lorry, (which was the last vehicle going on to the ferry), was involved in an accident. The watertight back doors of the boat came down on top of the container and punctured the roof. Because of the damage the insurers insisted that the lorry and container be taken off the ship and put into a safe compound overnight.

Unfortunately it rained rather heavily during the night and the rainwater reached the top layer of recorders which were nearest to the puncture in the container. They were sent back to the factory and the insurers condemned the whole container.

After lengthy negotiations, we obtained the lot, subject to the name being taken off the front of each machine. As the players were made for the Spanish market, we also had to change a chip in the machine to correspond with the British market. At this time, the usual price for these recorders was £399. When we put them on the market for £179 we had a constant stream of customers and we sold every one within two weeks. In the years since, we haven't had one complaint regarding the reliability of these machines and we are still using one ourselves nearly twenty years on!

Between 2000 and 2002 we looked at many interesting properties to continue building our portfolio, but because the market was rising at an alarming rate we lost out on a number of occasions due to some silly high prices being paid. We were quick off the mark when the adjoining property to our Sandy Bridge site came on the market. It had been a milk distribution depot for Cambrian United Dairies for as long as I can remember, and we made sure that we had it sewn up. We still have it in our portfolio and have licensed it to a small milk distribution company.

In March 2003, Patrick and I went on a buying trip to China. It seems that everything in the world is being produced in China at extremely good quality and prices and if one wants to stay competitive then one has to go there to see what is available. Our Contract Division in Sandy Bridge was already importing tables and chairs from Romania and Yugoslavia, so we decided to purchase stacking chairs and tables from China to extend our range. We have since been back out to China along with Vivian

Howard our Contracts Manager and purchased many containers of different types of furniture. So far we are extremely pleased with the service and quality of goods received and must say that they are extremely pleasant people to deal with.

The arrival of imported furniture from Romania and China.

September 2003 started quietly enough until I had a phone call from the Financial Director of one of the largest Upholstery Manufacturers in Britain. One of the Christie Tyler Group manufacturing for all the catalogue companies had 2,000 suites to clear and wanted to offer them to someone who would take the lot, at a price of £50 per suite. I went to the factory early the following morning and was amazed to see a very large storage warehouse with 3 piece suites stacked four high up to the roof. In ten minutes I had purchased the lot. The biggest problem was the fact that they wanted them all cleared within a month and at the time I didn't have a clue where I was going to put them.

Strange things always happen to me! The day after returning from the Furniture Factory I noticed a 'To Let' sign on a building quite close to us in Sandy Bridge. It was an old building of approximately 10,000 sq. ft. in a gated site of approximately two acres and over the previous thirty years it had been on lease to an electrical wholesaler called Weslec. In the 1950s' the Weslec site had been a railway wagon repair building and yard, owned at that time by an extraordinary man named Albie Evans. He was involved in numerous commercial dealings but his major one was a chain of 50 or so betting shops throughout the area. His son Karl (a friend of mine) took over the declining businesses after the death of his father, but a combination of high death duties and Karl's youth meant that most of them folded. When Karl opened a night club in Llanelli our Contracts Division had the opportunity to fully furnish it. Because I had allowed Karl time to repay me, I was issued with No. 1 of his Priority Club Membership cards. Sadly the club closed down after a few years but I still have that card to this day.

I approached Weslec and asked if I could rent the property which, since the company had moved out, was standing idle. A deal was done and I rented the site for six months. The trucks started turning up daily, and we had a special sale to clear as much as possible starting on the second week in October. By Christmas we had sold and delivered 1,500 3 piece suites, and we kept on selling them until it was necessary to purchase another 500 to keep the momentum going.

In the January 2004, I had had so many people stop and ask us if we had any spare space in the unit to rent that I came to the conclusion that if there was a chance then I must try to buy the freehold of this site so that I could develop it in any way that I wanted to. It took me another 15 months until I finally bought the whole site from the Stradey Estate. Now it was mine to do with it whatever I wanted to – subject to planning.

Years ago in 1981 I had purchased an old building and two acres of land in West Cross, Swansea. I bought it (50% each) with a personal friend named Terry Francis, who was a well known builder in and around Swansea. Llwyn Derw was sold to us by the company developing the site because at that time it was a listed building and they thought it would remain so. Our original intention was to turn it into a high class hotel, the most exclusive in Swansea, but because neither Terry nor I knew anything then about running a hotel, we decided to sit on it for a while. In fact we sat on it for 24 years! In the meantime, it was costing us a lot of money to police the building so we put a guard dog in to roam free. Vandals still got into the conservatory area and let the dog loose. They then got into the main building and over time they wrecked the artefacts inside and set a portion of it alight. Seven years later we had the building de-listed and flattened. The area was known as Llwyn Derw, West Cross. The house at one time had been owned by the Folland family and my mother had worked there in her younger days.

We sat on this property until 2003 and due to the ill health of Terry it was decided to sell the land. My son-in-law Johnathan is a builder and between us it was possible to purchase Terry's 50% of shares in the business and after months of problems we finally finished the first show house on the site and put that and the other five quality houses on the market in June 2004. Every house was sold in the first week of sales.

In June 2005 we applied for planning for building at our Weslec site. Patrick and Homestore are in the process of building a 15,000 sq. ft. building on our land at the rear of Homestore, Gorseinon, and apart from that there are one or two other things that could happen because it seems that things go pretty tame unless there are two or three balls in the air at one time.

Llwyn Derw.

In 2006, Maurice Clague Taylor died at the age of ninety two. He had been a lonely soul since his mother and sisters died and he had moved to a bungalow in Waunarlwydd. He regularly went roller-skating until he was eighty seven and when he had to give it up he told me he had nothing left to live for! I used to take him shopping for groceries, but after I had introduced him to Patrick he took to phoning him if he needed anything as he was closer at hand. After one shopping trip, he asked Patrick if he would like a cup of tea and then proceeded to fill the kettle with water from his rubber hot water bottle! He was recycling his water. After this, neither Patrick nor I felt tempted to share another cup of tea with him.

In September Cheryl and I were away in Memphis on a tour with the British Country Music Association and whilst in Nashville we were welcomed by the President of the Association George Hamilton IV. When Cheryl and I were talking to him and he found that we were from Wales, he sang 'We'll Keep a welcome in the hillside' especially for Cheryl.

George Hamilton IV with Cheryl.

On returning home we found that Maurice had died and his funeral had already taken place. He was an extraordinary character and I remember him with great affection. Maurice left me three of his oil paintings on canvas in his will as well as the photographs he and his sisters had taken at Llethryd. What a nice finish to a pleasant chapter in my life.

This is where we sell our contract furniture to clubs, pubs and hotels for the whole of South Wales. The Sales Director of this operation is Vivian Howard, and we import furniture mainly

Contracts division.

from China, Malaysia and Romania. We have both been out to China three times in the last four years. It is impossible to survive in the furniture contract business unless you buy from China. We have good suppliers and on the other hand – we are very good customers!

Vivian Howard with my very able P.A. Maureen Pilgrim, who has been with the company for many years.

130

We have owned the Tyre Depot property in Sandy Bridge for about twenty years. It has been let out to Goodyear tyres all that time.

Tyre depot – manager Phil Williams with Robert Nethercott and Brian Congdon.

In January 2008 we exchanged contracts on our Weslec site. It seems that a 'retirement home' company are building fifty flats in conjunction with two small retail units and are starting work there as soon as the planning is finalised. Thank goodness! One project less to think about!

The Weslec building and site which will be developed shortly.

131

Whilst awaiting planning consent, a local fair has set up at Weslec. Now that permission has been granted on the Stradey rugby grounds proposed development, the fair people (who had been using the grounds for over thirty years) had nowhere to go in the vicinity, so we have allowed them to use our site.

The Fairground on the Weslec site.

Our granddaughter Isabelle at the fair.

Chapter 8

MOTORS AND MEMORABILIA

Over the years, I have had three Rolls Royce. The first I bought from the owner of Mathews Paint Shop in Swansea, who lived in West Cross in the fine house that Bonnie Tyler and her husband Bobby now live. The second was a beautiful pale blue Camargue which I bought in Howells of Cardiff and my present one is a nice shade of mink and was bought from the County Sheriff of Haverfordwest who had had it from new. It is in my garage most of the time and last year we did 700 miles in total. It is not even a Sunday car!

Spike (Australia) and Cheryl with my blue Camargue.

Cheryl with the Silver Sprite.

I had bought an 'Iso Grifo' two-seater yellow Italian sports car in 1972, one of only eight in the country. The biggest problem with it was the fuel consumption of 9 miles to the gallon. The garage owner told me that one of its previous owners was named as one of Peter Sellers' companies. I never substantiated that and after five years I sold it to a friend near Chepstow and today it is very valuable.

The Iso Grifo.

Cheryl had always wanted a Mercedes sports car, so I searched around and bought her a 350 SL. I insured it even though it was going to be parked outside our house until I had had it road taxed the following month. We went to work in my car at 8. 50 a.m. and no sooner had we arrived in the office when there was a phone call from the wife of Bob Evans, our solicitor. She phoned to say that a tree had fallen in our driveway. I decided that it must be the small tree at the top of our driveway and went home to inspect.

I had the shock of my life because not only was it the biggest tree in our garden, but it had blown down where my car was usually parked and had crashed down on top of Cheryl's new car. If we had been 5 minutes later we could have been under the main trunk of the tree!

We were fully insured and no-one was hurt so there was no harm done.

We bought a white American stretch limo in 1998 after a visit to America. The limo was one of Donald Trump's Atlantic Casino Cars and it was bought from a photograph and shipped over in a container. I had great fun driving it around Gower and Llanelli and eventually I formed 'Long Limos' and we used the car for weddings and occasional hire for a couple of years.

My stretch limo in Llanrhidian.

We offered a trip in the limo as a first prize in a competition held by Llanrhidian Seniors, and George Tucker, Fritz Oltersdorf, Terry Williams and Bill Measday shared the prize.

George Tucker and Fritz Oltersdorf with their limo and chauffeur.

By kind permission of Betty Tanner.

On the 22nd December 1999, they were collected from their homes and taken to have a meal in our hotel – The Ashburnham Hotel in Pembrey. It was great to have them in my territory for a change, although I must say that for the last ten years we have regularly had the Llanrhidian Senior Citizens using our hotel on a day trip outing every November.

Terry Williams and Fritz Oltersdorf enjoy a celebratory drink.

By kind permission of Dulcie Oltersdorf.

Through the years I have purchased some interesting memorabilia at Charity Auctions. In 1979 local snooker player Terry Griffiths won the World Snooker Championship and was given the actual table on which he won the final. I purchased the table and it stands in my music room today. I was promised, at the time of purchase that a free lesson from Terry was included, but so far this hasn't come to fruition. I'm sure that if I asked him though, he would probably oblige.

The Duke and Duchess of Westminster were the original owners of 'The Blue Boy' by Thomas Gainsborough until it was sold to Harry Huntingdon (an American multi-billionaire) in

1921. This painting hangs in the Huntingdon Art Gallery in California, U.S.A. After the sale there must have been a space on the wall where the original had been, so the Duke and Duchess commissioned a fine artist to copy the original on panel. It was hung in a room in their Hill House estate at Wotten under Edge in Gloucester.

On the 24th October 1990, after the death of the Duchess, everything was put up for auction. Cheryl and I bought the painting at the auction and even though it is not the original we are still very fond of it.

My Blue Boy.

In 1995, experts in California used a stereo microscope and ultraviolet screening to probe the original and found that originally a white water spaniel had been painted standing by the Blue Boy's side. Gainsborough, in his wisdom had painted it out.

At a Cancer Charity event, we had the pleasure of bidding and winning a signed photograph of Sammy Davis Junior. It is ironic that the day that we bought it was the day that Sammy died. He had signed the photo "Peace. Sammy Davis Jnr."

Sammy Davis Jnr.

At the same auction we collected an autographed copy of Nancy Reagan's autobiographical memoirs "My Turn". It is a welcome addition to my library alongside an autographed tie by Ringo Starr and a signed photograph of Margaret Thatcher. We have various other celebrities' autographs but the most notable to date is a signed guitar by the Eagles. This was my wonderful 70th birthday present!

I also have an acre of land on the moon, a fabulous stand at the starting line position in this year's Grand Prix at Silverstone and a customised Gibson guitar to add to my musical collection.

We went to see Little Richard, the True King of Rock and Roll at St. David's Hall, Cardiff and what a show he put on! Little Richard from Macon, Georgia had tremendous hits with 'Tutti Frutti', 'Lucille', 'Long Tall Sally' and many more in 1957 and knowing this was probably the last chance to see him touring Britain – he's 75 years of age – we made sure that we had decent seats. We were invited to meet him after the show and after a half hour wait we had the pleasure of seeing him and shaking his hand. He had so much makeup, mascara and lipstick on and had had so many face lifts that I had a shock to see him close up. I remarked to him "Man, you look great!" and he answered politely "Well, thank you sir!"

Little Richard.

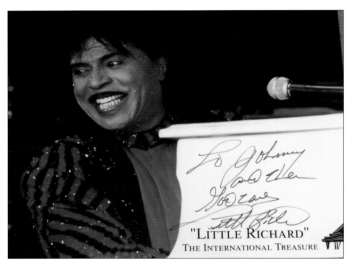

He signed a 3ft. by 2 ft. poster of himself with – To Johnny and Cheryl with love, Little Richard. He is a true giant of Rock and Roll!

I have supported a number of charities over the last thirty years and will continue to do so from a portion of the proceeds of this book.

Chapter 9

FULL CIRCLE

For my 60th birthday, Patrick had bought me a present of an old Telecaster electric guitar that had belonged to his cousin Eric. It is a beautiful guitar and since I hadn't touched a guitar for thirty five years and it was so much easier to handle than my old discarded one, I took to it immediately.

I turned an old snooker room in the house into a music room and before long we had a group put together and were rehearsing many times a week.

Rehearsing with Patrick and Kenny in our music room.

The 5 piece band was called 'Moonshine' and was a country band consisting of Cheryl – lead singer, me – guitarist and harmony singer, Bob – guitarist and very good lead singer, Alan – lead guitarist, Kenny – bass and backing singer and sometimes Patrick (rhythm guitar).

141

Moonshine: from left – Bob, Alan, Cheryl, me and Kenny.

Alan is a good lead guitarist from Port Talbot. He came into the band when John The Hat left. He is a school teacher.

Ken is a good bass guitarist and backing vocalist. He was one of the reasons that we put the band together. He lives in Llanelli and is retired, but spends every fine day flying his own plane from a private farm strip in Port Talbot. On rainy days you can find him drinking coffee in our warehouse in Llanelli – next door to his house!

Bob is an able guitarist and a fabulous lead singer.

Bob Leonard in fancy dress at the North Gower Hotel.

142

He is from Llansaint, Ferryside. We have been friends since he headed his own band over twenty five years ago. The first time that I met Bob was at a Fancy Dress night at the North Gower Hotel. At that time he was working during the day and entertaining at evening time.

He later had his own band at the North Gower and they were well liked by everybody. Some time later he and his wife June took over as managers of the hotel and were extremely popular hosts.

In our first five years together we played at various engagements but our aim was always to have fun and certainly not for profit.

On attaining the age of 60, I started writing songs again. There is so much satisfaction in knowing that you have written something that could be just as good as what is on the radio today.

My old Rocking Chair. ©

I've dug for silver; I've dug for gold,
I've searched for diamonds in mountains so cold
I've got plenty of money, rich beyond compare,
And I've stuffed it in the mattress of my old rocking chair.

The cover is dirty and nearly worn through
With springs sticking out with horse hair and glue
A tapestry blanket helps cover the wear
But everyone knows it's **my** rocking chair.

The ladies surround me 'cos they know I've got bread
Keeping me sweet 'cos they like me – it's said
But as I get older and losing my hair
I sit myself firmly on my rocking chair.

I finally go to the sky – like a dove
Watching my chair from way up above
And horror of horrors – to my great despair
Sian's given Guy Fawkes my old rocking chair!

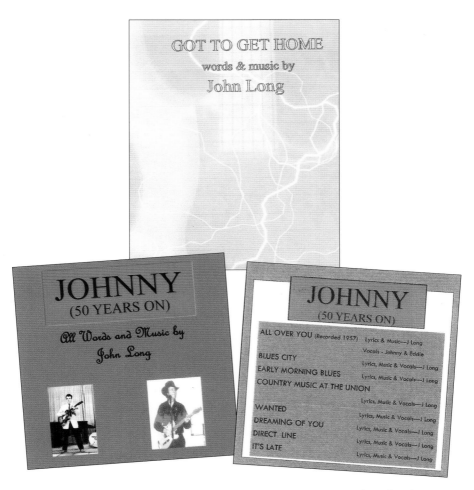

I'm not sure where we go from here. Events tend to lead into other events. I suppose that is what business is all about, especially when you have diversified as much as we have done.

In April 2007 we finally completed the purchase of a 60 acre farm in Gower. We had been keeping an eye on all the Gower residential sales for the last five years and when we got to know that the old, dilapidated farm and land might come onto the market we tracked the owners down in Bath and after a year of negotiations we managed to persuade them to sell to us rather than put it on the market. It is a wonderful spot and we feel that we are so lucky to have it.

The pillory on the village green.

In July, Cheryl and I made a 'musical' contribution to Llanrhidian Fair. The villagers had organised an old fashioned village fair with a pillory on the village green near the old 'Whipping Stone'.

They also decided to decorate the village with scarecrows of different characters. We, of course, chose to make Elvis.

Elvis.

August 2007 was my 70th birthday and it was decided that we would go to Las Vegas, to celebrate the event with our staff and friends. A few close friends couldn't make it for various reasons but we still had a party of twenty five of us for the special event.

Las Vegas trip. Included here are – Patrick & Jeanette Pattison, Bob & Jennifer Evans, Viv & Marie Howard, Sian & Jonathon Hale Quant, Jackie & David Quant, Peter & Helen Evans, Ken Evans, John & Cheryl Long, Rino & Cynthia Renesto, Maureen & Graham Pilgrim.

We were taken by stretch limos from Las Vegas airport to our hotel 'The Flamingo' on the Strip, and had a great time, culminating with a party at the Golden Nugget on Saturday the 18th – my birthday. So we were having a re-run of the trips that we used to do with the staff over thirty years ago.

Nicole arrived in her private jet to join in the celebrations.

Nicole in her private jet.

Nicole went on another shopping spree in Las Vegas. This time Patrick was the 'packhorse'. If you haven't been shopping with a multi-millionairess – then you haven't lived! She is however a very generous person, as all of the purchases were gifts for her friends!

The first half of 2007 was probably my most creative time for song writing. It was rather strange because I went through a period of waking up in the middle of the night with a song in my head, I would put the words together with the rhyming and all the chord sequences and tell myself that I will remember them all first thing in the morning. By the following morning I could not remember a thing of what I had thought was so great four hours before. So I sorted out that problem by having pen and paper on my bedside cabinet and on the next occasion (four o'clock in the morning) I got up and crept to my bathroom further down the landing and put the song down complete without waking Cheryl.

Between March and June was my most prolific time when I wrote about twenty songs. I decided to record seven songs for posterity. Cheryl, Kenny and I recorded them on a small 8 track recording studio that we have in the house and gave our production to a friend Tim Hamill of 'Sonic Sound' who tidied them up and put them on a disc for us. I was pleased with the result.

After my 70th birthday in Vegas and the success of my first recordings for fifty years, I decided to put down on paper some of the things that have happened to me during my lifetime – hence this book!

Seventy years is a long time to remember everything that has happened and if I have deviated slightly from the actual, or if I have left out some of the many people and friends that have helped me on the way then I apologise and lay the blame on my AGE!